THE SMART INSTANT POT COOKBOOK FOR BEGINNERS

Easy & Most Delicious Instant Pot Recipes Made For Your Everyday Cooking with Beginners Guide.

BY

Francis Michael

ISBN: 978-1-952504-44-0

COPYRIGHT © 2020 by Francis Michael

All rights reserved. This book is copyright protected and it's for personal use only. Without the prior written permission of the publisher, no part of this publication should be reproduced, distributed, or transmitted in any form or by any means, including photocopying, recording, or other electronic or mechanical methods.

This book is sold with the idea that the author is not needed to render accounting, officially permitted, or otherwise, qualified services. It's recommended to seek for the services of a legal or professional, a practiced individual in the profession if advice is needed.

DISCLAIMER

The information written in this publication is geared for educational and entertainment purposes only. Concerted efforts have been made towards providing accurate, up to date and reliable complete information. The information in this book is true and complete to the best of our knowledge.

Neither the publisher nor the author takes any responsibility for any possible consequences of reading or enjoying the recipes in this book. The author and publisher disclaim any liability in connection with the use of information contained in this book. Under no circumstance will any legal responsibility or blame be apportioned against the author or publisher for any reparation, damages, or monetary loss due to the information herein, either directly or indirectly.

Table of Contents

CHAPTER 1: KNOW YOUR INSTANT POT 7

    What is Instant Pot? 7

Reasons Why You need An Instant Pot 8

How To Use The Buttons 10

Step-by-Step Guide to Effectively Clean Your Instant Pot 14

Instant Pot Must Have Tools 16

CHAPTER 2: BREAKFAST RECIPES 17

    Banana Oatmeal 17

    Sweet Potato Morning Hash 18

    Jamaican Cornmeal Porridge 19

    Rice Pudding 20

    Vanilla Apple Cinnamon Breakfast Quinoa 21

    Easy Apple Butter 22

    Buckwheat Porridge 23

    Quinoa Blueberry Breakfast Bowl 24

    Oatmeal 25

CHAPTER 3: EGG RECIPES 26

    French "Baked" Eggs 26

    Bacon and Egg Risotto 27

    Mexican Egg Casserole 28

    Egg Bake 29

    Western Omelet Quiche 31

    Cheesy Egg Bake 32

    Spanish Tortilla Potato Egg Frittata, Quiche 33

    Crustless Veggie Quiche 35

CHAPTER 4: POULTRY RECIPES 36

Thai Chicken Rice Bowl 36

Creamy Chicken Noodle Soup 38

Buffalo Chicken Lettuce Wraps 39

Chipotle Chicken Black Beans and Rice 40

Chicken Breasts.. 41

Pulled Tandoori Chicken 42

Cashew Butter Chicken 44

Lemon Garlic Chicken 45

Honey Curry Chicken 46

Italian Chicken 47

CHAPTER 5: FISH & SEAFOODS.. 48

Creamy Fish Chowder 48

Shrimp and Lentil Stew 49

Coconut Red Curry Shrimp... 50

Fish Stew.. 52

Salmon.. 54

Shrimp 55

Lemon Pepper Salmon 56

Drunken Clams... 57

Mussels 58

Shrimp Paella 59

Spicy Pineapple Shrimp.. 61

Savory Shrimp with Tomatoes and Feta.. 62

Creamy Chipotle Shrimp Soup 63

CHAPTER 6: BEEF RECIPES... 65

Homemade Hamburger 65

Cheesesteak Sloppy 66

- Beef and Macaroni 67
- Spaghetti 69
- Goulash 70
- Stuffed Pepper Casserole 71
- Taco Meat 72
- Vegetable Beef Soup 73
- Sweet Potato Chili 74
- Beef Stroganoff 75
- Bolognese 76
- Picadillo 77
- Mongolian Beef 78

CHAPTER 7: PORK RECIPES 79
- Ground Pork Casserole 79
- Pork Chops with Gravy 80
- Pulled Pork 82
- Pork Chili 83
- Pork Green Chili 85
- Spicy Pork & Spinach Stew 86
- Pork Stew with Fall Vegetables 87
- Pozole (Pork and Hominy Stew) 88
- Coca-Cola Pulled Pork 89

CHAPTER 8: APPETIZERS 91
- Salsa 91
- Sweet and Spicy Meatballs 92
- Hawaiian Meatballs 93
- White Queso Dip 94
- Cheddar Bacon Ale Dip 95

Buffalo Chicken Dip 96

Crispy Chicken Wings 98

Stuffed Peppers 99

Potato Corn Chowder 100

Apple Pie Steel Cut Oats 101

Creamy Macaroni and Cheese 102

CHAPTER 9: SOUPS & STEWS 103

Minestrone Soup 103

Pot Borscht (Beet Soup) 105

Chicken Noodle Soup 106

Chicken Meatball and Kale Soup 108

Paleo Hamburger Soup 110

Egg Roll Soup 111

Thai Peanut Chicken Soup 112

Beef Stew with Potatoes 113

CHAPTER 1: KNOW YOUR INSTANT POT

What is Instant Pot?

The Instant Pot Is One Programmable Machine That Does the Work of 7 Gadgets. Instant Pot is a seven-in-one multi-cooker that works as an electric pressure cooker, slow cooker, rice cooker, yogurt maker, steamer, warmer, and sauté pan all in one. Instant Pot is a multi-cooker that offers the same functionalities you'd find in a slow cooker, electric pressure cooker, rice cooker, steamer, yogurt maker, sauté/browning pan, and warming pot. It cooks meals faster, and offers the option for a delayed programmable start time.

The Instant Pot has a lot of functionality for one appliance, and at a decent price point. Most of all, I love the convenience. I can set it and walk away, and it saves time cooking foods like dried beans, lentils, whole grains, and stew. It's also durable and easy to clean. With so much functionality it can feel a little overwhelming and intimidating to learn how to use it. The electric pressure cooker function works at a lower maximum pressure than stovetop pressure cookers (which operate at 15 psi). This isn't specific to Instant Pot, however; it's true of all electric pressure cookers. Many pressure cooker recipes are written assuming the higher 15 psi pressure, so a few minutes of additional cook time may need to be added when using the Instant Pot.

Anyone who wants to own a slow cooker, pressure cooker, and rice cooker, but doesn't have the space to store all three, and who values quick, convenient cooking, and the "set it and forget it" aspect of slow cookers would love Instant Pot. Instant Pot comes with an instruction manual and short booklet of recipes. While basic and brief, the instruction manual covers all of Instant Pot's functions, as well as the recommended ratio of ingredients (like grains and dried beans) to water, and the cook times for popular items.

Reasons Why You need An Instant Pot

1. **Cook Beans Super Fast:**

This is the first thing that piqued my interest. I heard that people were cooking beans in as little as 10-15 minutes for soaked beans and as long as 35-40 minutes for dry beans. Since it normally took several hours to slow cook beans this got my attention. I was really concerned that this was another single use appliance so I wasn't won over yet. Then I heard it again and again. People I really admire were in love with their Instant Pot and it officially landed on my wish list.

2. **Make Perfect Brown Rice:**

I've always thought that rice was really easy to cook. I know some people really struggle with it but it was easy for me. The first time I made brown rice in the Instant Pot I read and re-read the grain to water ratio. I was puzzled because it used less water and I was worried I would get crunchy rice. Guess what, it wasn't crunchy it was perfect! Perhaps the most perfect rice I've ever made with just the right amount of "stickiness."

Previously when I would have a busy day I'd cook rice in my Crock Pot. We love the Mexican Casserole and Cheezy Broccoli and Rice Casserole but some readers found it too mushy. The Instant Pot made these recipes perfectly in a fraction of the time. No more mushy rice.

3. **Steam/Cook Veggies in Minutes:**

When I hold local classes I usually admit that my method of cooking is to start cooking, walk away and forget I'm cooking, smell the food later then go back to the stove to check on it. That is why all of my recipes are so simple and easy. I've burned more than my fair share of veggies by forgetting about them. The Instant Pot cooks veggies in minutes. Just be sure to release the steam once they are finished cooking.

4. **Built in Timer:**

My favorite thing about Crock Pots is that you can leave and come back to fully cooked meals. My Instant Pot goes one step further. It has a timer so it won't start cooking until I want it to. Dinner doesn't have to start cooking in the morning and cook all day. You can program it to begin dinner at 4:30 and keep it warm until you get home.

Even if you are home during the day think about how much time you will save by setting it up during a spare moment and not thinking about it again until dinner time.

5. **Easy Clean Up:**

My least favorite thing to do in the kitchen is washing dishes. If I could outsource it, I totally would. Sometimes I don't cook a specific meal because I don't want to do the dishes. The Instant Pot is really easy to clean up. It comes with a big stainless steel pot and a lid. That is all you have to wash and it's really easy.

6. **Pressure Cooking Retains More Nutrients:**

This one I'll have to leave to the experts but I've read that pressure cooking retains more nutrients because foods cook for a shorter amount of time and less water is used. Due to the high pressure, beans and grains become more digestible. So, if you've avoided beans and grains due to stomach issues this MAY help. (I'm not a doctor or scientist so don't eat something that could make you sick.)

7. **They are Safe:**

You and I have all heard crazy stories of pressure cookers blowing up. I've resisted pressure cookers in the past because they scared me. The Instant Pot is safe! There are 10 safety features built-in to the Instant Pot including automatic pressure control, high temperature warning, and a lid that locks while pressurized plus many more.

8. **Slow Cooker:**

The Instant Pot is roughly the same size as my slow cooker (it's a little taller) but it does the same job with the touch of a button. If you plan to use your Instant Pot as a slow cooker regularly be sure to purchase the optional lid.

9. **Sauté Feature:**

The Instant Pot can also sauté with the touch of a button. So you can toss onions and garlic in, select sauté, get the rest of your ingredients ready and then add them to the pot and program it to make Soup or whatever else your heart desires.

How To Use The Buttons

1. **Manual / Pressure Buttons:**

This is probably going to be the buttons you use most on the Instant Pot. It will allow you to pressure cook and manually select the time you want – rather than the preset buttons (such as Soup/Stew or Meat buttons). You can adjust the pressure, temperature and time by selecting the "+/-" buttons. Be sure to follow recipes (and add at least 1/2 cup to 1 cup of liquid to the inner pot) and note whether meals should be cooked at low or high pressure. The Instant Pot does default to High Pressure when the "Manual" button is selected, so adjust accordingly. And remember that the "Manual" / "Pressure" buttons are for pressure cooking – not for other functions like sauté, yogurt making or slow cooker (which don't require pressure cooking)

High Pressure

10.2 to 11.6 psi

239°F to 244°F

Low Pressure

5.8 to 7.2 psi

229 to 233°F

Note: The newer models of the Instant Pot have the same feature – it's called the "Pressure Cook" button.

2. **Sauté Button:**

The "Sauté" Button is the second most used function with my Instant Pot. You can do that and basically cook up anything as you would in a skillet or pan. You don't need the 1 cup of liquid. Just press the "Sauté" button, add some cooking oil (I like avocado or coconut) or animal fat like beef tallow or lard to the inner pot and add food you want to cook like a skillet or pan.

You can even adjust the sauté temperature:

Normal mode: 320 to 349°F

More mode: 347 to 410°F

Less mode: 275 to 302°F

I often start with the "Sauté" function and then use the "Manual" / "Pressure" button to then pressure cook my meal. It's fantastic to be able to use one pot for easy clean-up.

3. **Slow Cook Button:**

Use your Instant Pot like a slower cooker with this option. Just add food as you normally would to a slow cooker, close the lid (or use a slow cooker lid) and then press the "Slow Cook" button.

It will default to a 4-hour slow cook time. You can use "+/-" buttons to adjust the cook time.

4. **Bean / Chili:**

One of my favorite things to make in the Instant Pot is beans. It's so much faster (and tastier) with the Instant Pot. When you use the "Bean / Chili" button, it will default to a High Pressure for 30 minutes. You can adjust for "More" to High Pressure for 40 minutes or "Less" for High Pressure for 25 minutes. Typically, black beans take about 10-15 minutes, while kidney beans take 20-25. Refer to the Instant Pot Manual for cooking times for various beans and legumes. My Homemade Chili normally takes about 2-3 hours in the slow cooker, but with the Instant Pot it's just 25 minutes. I use a Natural Release for 5-10 minutes.

5. **Meat / Stew:**

Make your favorite stew or meat dish in the Instant Pot. Adjust the settings depending on the texture you want. For instance, the "More" setting is better for fall-off-the-bone cooking. It will default to a High Pressure for 35 minutes. You can adjust for "More" to High Pressure for 45 minutes or "Less" for High Pressure for 20 minutes. For a homemade stew with about 1-2 lb. of meat, I typically set to "Meat / Stew" in the Normal setting (high pressure for 35 minutes) and Natural Release for 10 minutes.

6. **Multigrain:**

The "Multigrain" button is best for cooking brown rice and wild rice, which typically takes longer than white rice to cook. Cook brown rice to a 1:1.25 ratio rice to water and wild rice to a 1:3 ratio rice to water for 22-30 minutes.

It will default at the "Normal" setting is 40 minutes of pressure cooking time. Adjust as needed for the "Less" setting is 20 minutes of pressure cooking time, or "More" at 45 minutes of warm water soaking and 60 minutes of pressure cooking.

7. **Porridge:**

Use the "Porridge" button to make rice porridge (congee) and other grains (not regular white or brown rice). It will default to a High Pressure for 20 minutes, which is best for rice porridge. You can adjust for "More" to High Pressure for 30 minutes or "Less" for High Pressure for 15 minutes. After the porridge is finished, do not use the QR handle. Because it has a high starch content, using the QR will splatter the porridge through the steam release vent. Use the Natural Rrelease.

8. **Poultry:**

Make your favorite chicken recipes with the "Poultry" button with the Instant Pot. It will default to a High Pressure for 15 minutes. You can adjust for "More" to High Pressure for 30 minutes or "Less" for High Pressure for 5 minutes.

I love to make shredded chicken for homemade tacos and burrito bowls. Add about 1 lb. uncooked chicken, 1/2 onion, 1 clove garlic minced, 1 cup bone broth, 1 tsp cumin, 1/2 tsp oregano, 1/8 tsp paprika, and 1/4 cup homemade salsa. Place lid on and set to "Poultry" to the default at High Pressure for 15 minutes. NR for 10 minutes and then QR. Open lid, use a fork and tongs to shred chicken and add salt and pepper to taste.

9. **Rice:**

You can cook rice in the Instant Pot in nearly half the time as a conventional rice cooker. White rice, short grain, Jasmine and Basmati rice can all be cooked on this setting in about 4 to 8 minutes. In general, you'll need a 1:1 ratio of rice to water (Basmati is a 1:1.5 ratio). When you choose the "Rice" button, the cooking duration automatically adjusts depending on how much food you put into the unit and cook on low pressure. Be sure to add about 10-12 minutes to the total cooking time to allow the Instant Pot to come to pressure.

Personally, I prefer to cook rice in the "Manual" mode at high pressure. I add 1:1 ratio of rice to water to the Instant Pot and set to 3 minutes with a 12 minutes Natural Release.

10. **Soup:**

Use the "Soup" button to make broth, stock or soup. The Instant Pot will control the pressure and temperature so that the liquid doesn't heavily boil. You can adjust the cooking time as needed, typically between 20-40 minutes, and the pressure to either low or high. Make a homemade bone broth WAY faster than the conventional slow cooker. Select the "Soup" button, set the pressure to low, and set the cooking time to 120 minutes. Once it's done, let the bone broth Natural Release for about an hour.

11. **Steam:**

Use the "Steam" button to steam vegetables, seafood or reheat food (it's a great alternative to the microwave). Be sure to use the steam rack included with the Instant Pot, otherwise food may burn and stick to the bottom of the inner pot.

Add 1-2 cups of water to the inner pot, place the steam rack inside the inner pot and with a stainless steel steam basket on top. Add vegetables, seafood, etc. in the basket. Press the "Steam" button and then adjust the time using the "+" or "-" key. Foods like frozen corn on the cob or a fresh fish filet will take 3-5 minutes, while fresh artichokes could take 9-11 minutes. Refer to the Instant Pot Manual for cooking times for various foods. Make homemade yogurt in the Instant Pot with glass bottles (such as Mason jars).

It's basically a 2-step process:

- Add milk to glass containers. Add 1 cup water to the inner pot, put in steam wrap and place glass containers filled with milk on top of the steam rack. Select the

"Steam" function and set the time for 1 minute. Use NR. Keep the water in the inner pot.
- Let the milk cool below 115°F and then add yogurt starter or yogurt from another batch (or store-bought). Press the "Yogurt" button and adjust to "Normal" mode and adjust time based on your recipe. When the yogurt is done, it will display "yogurt".

12. **Keep Warm / Cancel Button:**

Once the Instant Pot is done cooking, you can use the "Keep Warm" / "Cancel" function to keep food hot or to cancel the pressure cooking mode.

- **Keep Warm Button:**

When pressure cooking is done, the Instant Pot will beep and automatically go into the "Keep Warm" function. It will display an "L" in front of a number to indicate how long it's been warm – e.g. "L0:30" for 30 minutes. It's a great feature to keep food warm (145 to 172°F) for up to 99 hours, 50 minutes. It's perfect for pot lucks.

- **Cancel Button:**

At any time, you can cancel cooking and return to standby mode by pressing the "Keep Warm" / "Cancel" button. This is a great option if you selected the wrong time for pressure cooking and need to stop to make adjustments to the pressure or time.

13. **Timer Button:**

Use the Timer button to delay the cooking start time for the Instant Pot. This works for both pressure cooking and slow cook options.

To use this feature, just press the Timer button with 10 seconds of pressing either the Pressure / Manual button or Slow Cook button. Use "+/-" buttons to adjust the delayed hours, then wait a second and press Timer again to set delayed minutes. You can cancel the Timer anytime by pressing the Keep Warm / Cancel button.

Step-by-Step Guide to Effectively Clean Your Instant Pot

Step 1: Unplug

First things first, make sure your Instant Pot is unplugged before you start cleaning. It's a good idea to unplug your Instant Pot whenever it's not in use, but on this occasion in particular, you'll want to make sure it's unplugged for the intensive cleaning you're about to do, both for your safety and also for the safety of your appliance.

Step 2: Cleaning housing unit

While the outside housing unit definitely can't go in the dishwasher, you should be able to clean it thoroughly with a rag. Get the rag good and damp with water and cleaning solution, and wipe down both the inside and outside of the main housing unit (the exterior of the appliance, which holds the inner pot). For an even more thorough cleaning, use a sponge to get those hard-to-remove food bits and mineral deposits. Don't forget the nooks and crannies where little particles like to lodge!

Step 3: Wash lid

Next, you'll want to give the lid a good wash. You can hand-wash it in the sink with warm water, and be sure to add a little dish soap to make sure you're removing any and all bacteria and other nasty things you definitely don't want in your food. You might need to use a vinegar solution to get rid of all residual smells.

Step 4: Check other crevices

The Instant Pot has some nooks and crannies that you might not think to clean all the time. Now is the time to get all those crevices and small parts where food residue may build up over time. Remove the Quick Release handle, and wash it with warm, soapy water. Check around the steam valve, which can get blocked if too much deposit builds up there. Remove the shield, located inside the lid, which blocks the valve. Depending on the model you own, the shield could pop off easily, or it may need to be unscrewed. Check your owner's manual, or play around with it unless you've removed it. Wash the shield in the sink. Lastly, take a look at the condensation collection cup, which should be located on the side of your appliance. It may have collected food residue over time, so give it a scrubbing in the sink if it looks like it needs a cleaning.

Step 5: clean sealing ring

The silicone ring that can be found on the underside of the lid will likely need a thorough cleaning. After all, that's what ensures your Instant Pot has a tight seal, and it's an easy spot for food particles or residual smells to lurk. You should also check it for any signs of damage, as silicone can start to crack over time. If you notice any tears in the silicone ring, you'll want to order a replacement immediately. The silicone ring is dishwasher-safe, so you can pop it in there on the top rack. Once it's thoroughly cleaned, place it back on the underside of the lid, and make sure you've got a secure fit.

Step 6: Wash the inner pot

The inner pot is dishwasher-safe, so you should be washing this regularly anyway. But since you're doing a deep clean, it doesn't hurt to pop the inner pot into the dishwasher, along with any of the other dishwasher-safe accessories you use with your Instant Pot, such as silicone molds and wire racks. Once the inner pot is out of the dishwasher, dry it off with a paper towel and use some household vinegar to give it a thorough wipe-down. This gets rid of any built-up residue from things like minerals in your water, or dish detergent. After all, you want your Instant Pot to look nice and shiny, don't you? This will help with any smells as well.

Step 7: Steam clean and let dry

Now that everything is clean, you can reassemble everything. Don't forget about those small, easy-to-miss pieces, like the sealing ring and shield. Those are extra important to ensure you're using your Instant Pot safely, so definitely don't forget about them. Just in case the sealing ring still has a strange food smell, you can go a step further and deodorize the part with a vinegar steam clean. It's a simple process and can be done directly in the Instant Pot. Just add one cup of water, one cup of vinegar, and some lemon peels (for extra freshness!) to the inner pot, and run the Instant Pot's "Steam" setting for a few minutes. Be sure to allow pressure to release naturally, and when the lid is safe to open, you can remove the sealing ring and let it dry on the kitchen counter.

Instant Pot Must Have Tools

1. **Sealing ring:** There is a silicone ring inside of the lid. This ring can last for about 6 to 18 months. You have to separate the sealing rings for sweet and savory foods because the ring can retain strong odors.

2. **Glass lid:** The pressure cooker has tempered glass lids that are good for slow-cooker setting so you can see the food in the pot.

3. **Round cake pans and casserole dishes:** The pressure cooker has a 7inch round spring form pan for cheesecake, 7-inch cake pans, and 1½ quart soufflé or ramekins that will fit inside the pressure cooking pot. The large capacity Instant Pots can hold larger sizes. It is important to always measure and check to see if the pan or dish fits.

4. **Mini silicone oven mitts:** The pressure cooker has a mini silicone oven. You can use any oven mitts, but I will recommend the miniature ones because they handy for safely gripping the lid of the very hot inner pot.

5. **Steaming baskets:** Expandable metal steamer baskets, silicone or wire mesh can be used. The steamer basket can be used to keep hard-boiled eggs or steam veggies foods off the bottom of the Instant Pot. You can use the steamer basket when making broth and keep your bones in the basket for easy straining afterward.

CHAPTER 2: BREAKFAST RECIPES

Banana Oatmeal

Preparation time: 5 minutes

Cooking time: 20 minutes

Total time: 25 minutes

Serves: 2

Ingredients

- 1 cup of water
- 1 cup of milk (we used 1% fat milk)
- ½ cup of steel cut oats
- ¼ tsp. of cinnamon powder
- ½ of a large banana, mashed
- 1 to 2 tbsp of brown sugar, adjust to taste
- Splash of vanilla extract

Cooking Instructions

1. Spray the inner liner of your Instant Pot with a non-stick spray.

2. Add the water, milk, steel cut oats, cinnamon powder. Place the mashed banana on top and don't stir.

3. Close and lock the lid in place and ensure that the valve is in sealing position. Select the "Porridge" function and set the time to 15 minutes.

4. When the timer beeps, use a quick pressure release. Carefully remove the lid and give everything a good stir.

5. Add the brown sugar (or your desired sweetener). Give everything a good mix until combined. Add a splash of vanilla extract and mix again.

6. Place the banana oatmeal into individual platter and top with sliced bananas, peanut butter, sliced almonds or your desired topping.

7. Serve and enjoy!

Sweet Potato Morning Hash

Preparation time: 10 mins

Cooking time: 10 mins

Total time: 20 mins

Servings: 4

Ingredients

- 6 large eggs
- 1 tbsp. of Italian seasoning
- ½ tsp. of sea salt
- ½ tsp. of ground black pepper
- ½ lb. of ground pork sausage
- 1 large sweet potato, peeled and cubed
- 1 small onion, peeled and diced
- 2 cloves of garlic, minced
- 1 medium green bell pepper, seeded and diced
- 2 cups of water

Cooking Instructions

1. Whisk eggs, Italian seasoning, pepper and salt together in a medium bowl and set aside

2. Press the Sauté button on your Instant Pot. Stir-fry sausage, sweet potato, onion, garlic, and bell pepper together for 3 to 5 minutes until onions are translucent.

3. Put the mixture to a 7-cup greased glass dish and pour the whisked eggs over the sausage mixture.

4. Place steamer rack in your Instant Pot and pour in water.

5. Place dish with egg mixture onto steamer rack. Close the lid and ensure that the valve is in sealing position

6. Select Manual function to cook on High-Pressure for about 5 minutes.

7. When timer beeps, do a quick pressure release until float valve drops. then open the lid carefully.

8. Remove dish from Instant Pot. Let sit at room temperature for 4 to 10 minutes to allow the eggs to set properly. Serve and enjoy

Jamaican Cornmeal Porridge

Preparation time: 5 minutes

Cooking Time: 20 minutes

Total Time: 25 minutes

Serves: 4

Ingredients

- 4 cups of water, separated
- 1 cup of milk
- 1 cup of yellow cornmeal, fine
- 2 sticks cinnamon
- 3 pimento berries
- 1 teaspoon of vanilla extract
- ½ teaspoon of nutmeg, ground
- ½ cup of sweetened condensed milk

Cooking Instructions

1. First, set your Instant Pot on porridge setting for 6 minutes.

2. Put 3 cups of water and 1 cup of milk to your Instant Pot.

3. Whisk 1 cup of water and cornmeal properly in a separate bowl, Add to your instant pot and whisk.

4. Put cinnamon sticks, pimento berries, nutmeg and vanilla extract. Cover the Lid and allow to cook for 6 minutes.

5. When time is up, use a natural pressure release and allow to release pressure.

6. Once done with natural pressure release, then add sweetened condensed milk to sweeten.

7. Serve and enjoy.

Rice Pudding

Preparation time: 5

Cooking time: 35

Total time: 40 minutes

Serves: 4

Ingredients

- 1 cup of short grain brown rice
- 1 ½ cups of water
- 1 tablespoon of vanilla extract
- 1 cinnamon Stick
- 1 tablespoon of butter
- 1 cup of raisins
- 3 tablespoons of Honey
- ½ cup Heavy Cream

Cooking Instructions

1. Put rice, water, vanilla, cinnamon stick, and butter into your Instant Pot and close the Lid.

2. Select the Manual button of your Instant Pot and set time to 20 minutes.

3. When time is up, allow pressure to release naturally. Remove the cinnamon stick and discard. Stir in raisins, honey and cream.

4. Select sauté button on your Instant Pot, then select Adjust button to change the temperature to Less and simmer for about 5 minutes.

5. Serve Warm and enjoy.

Vanilla Apple Cinnamon Breakfast Quinoa

Preparation time: 5 minutes

Cooking time: 1 minutes

Total time: 6 minutes

Serves: 4

Ingredients

- 1 cup of quinoa
- 1 ½ cup of water
- ¼ teaspoon of mineral salt
- 1 chopped apple
- 2 tablespoons of cinnamon
- ½ teaspoon of vanilla
- ¼ cup gentle sweet

Cooking Instructions

1. put all ingredients to your Instant Pot and stir thoroughly.
2. Cover and lock the Lid.
3. Select Manual function to cook on High-Pressure for about 1 minute.
4. When time is up, do a natural pressure release for about 8 minutes.
5. Then open the Lid carefully and serve.

Easy Apple Butter

Preparation time: 15 mins

Cooking time: 1 hour

Total time: 1 hour 15 mins

Ingredients

- 5 pounds of apples
- ½ cup of brown sugar
- ¼ teaspoon of ground cloves
- ½ teaspoon of ground nutmeg
- 1 tablespoon of cinnamon
- pinch of salt
- 2 tablespoons of apple cider vinegar
- 1 tablespoon of vanilla extract
- ¼ cup water

Cooking Instructions

1. Add all the ingredients in your pressure cooker and mix them properly.
2. Close and lock the Lid in place.
3. Select Manual function to cook on High-Pressure for about 1 hour.
4. Allow the pressure cooker to release pressure naturally and carefully remove the Lid.
5. Use the immersion blender to blend the apple smoothly, then pour into the jar.
6. Keep the apple butter for about 3 weeks in the refrigerator.
7. Serve and enjoy.

Buckwheat Porridge

Prep Time: 5 minutes

Cook Time: 25 minutes

Total Time: 30 minutes

Serves: 4 to 5

Ingredients

- 1 cup of raw buckwheat groats
- 3 cups of rice milk
- 1 banana sliced
- ¼ cup raisins
- 1 teaspoon of ground cinnamon
- 1/2 teaspoon. vanilla
- chopped nuts optional

Cooking Instructions

1. Rinse buckwheat and put in your Instant Pot.

2. Put rice milk, banana, raisins, vanilla and cinnamon. Close and lock the Lid in place.

3. Ensure that the steam release is in the closed position.

4. Select Manual function to cook on High-Pressure for about 6 minutes.

5. When time is up, turn off the pot and allow time for the natural pressure release for about 20 minutes.

6. After pressure is released, carefully open the Lid of your Instant Pot and stir porridge with a long-handled spoon.

7. Put more rice milk to individual servings to achieve preferred consistency.

8. Sprinkle with chopped nuts if desired.

9. Serve and enjoy.

Quinoa Blueberry Breakfast Bowl

Preparation time: 5 minutes

Total time: 5 minutes

Serves: 4

Ingredients

- 1 ½ cups of white quinoa
- 1 ½ cups of water
- 1 cinnamon stick
- ¼ cup of raisins
- 1 tbsp of honey plus more for serving
- ¾ cup of grated apple
- 1 cup of cold-pressed apple juice
- 1 cup of plain yogurt plus more for serving
- ¼ cup of chopped pistachios
- Blueberries to serve

Cooking Instructions

1. Use a fine mesh strainer to rinse the quinoa. Put the quinoa, cinnamon stick and water to your Instant Pot.

2. Close and lock the Lid in place, make sure the vent is set to sealing.

3. Select Manual function to cook on High-Pressure for about 1 minute.

4. When time is up, allow the pressure release naturally for about 10 minutes and then do a quick pressure release.

5. Transfer the quinoa into a medium size bowl, then remove the cinnamon stick and allow to cool.

6. Put the, honey, raisins, apple and apple juice and stir to combine properly. Then refrigerate for 1 hour.

7. Put the yogurt and stir to combine.

8. Serve topped with yogurt, pistachios, blueberries and honey.

9. Enjoy.

Oatmeal

Prep Time: 5 mins

Cook Time: 5 mins

Total Time: 10 mins

Serves: 4

Ingredients

- 1 cup of oats (use steel oats if you like)
- 2 ½ cup of water
- 1 cup of apple skinned and diced
- 2 tablespoons of brown sugar
- 3 tablespoons of butter
- Pinch of cinnamon
- raisins optional

Cooking Instructions

1. Set your Instant Pot on Manual High Pressure.

2. Put butter and allow to melt. Then, turn off your instant pot.

3. Put, water, oats, brown sugar, apples, cinnamon and raisins if desired.

4. Stir the ingredients properly. Close the Lid and the steam valve, set to manual high pressure for 5 minutes.

5. When time is up, do a quick release.

6. Serve and enjoy.

CHAPTER 3: EGG RECIPES

French "Baked" Eggs

Preparation time: 6 mins

Cooking time: 8 mins

Total time: 14 mins

Ingredients

- 4 eggs
- 4 slices of meat, fish or vegetables
- 4 slices of cheese, or shot of cream
- 4 garnish of fresh herbs
- olive oil

Cooking Instructions

1. Add one cup of water on the trivet of your pressure cooker and set aside.

2. Prepare the ramekins by adding a drop of olive oil in each and rubbing the bottom and sides.

3. After rubbing the olive oil, lay a slice of preferred meat or vegetable.

4. Break an egg and drop it into the ramekin. Then, put sliced cheese, or cream, of your choice.

5. For a soft egg yolk, cover properly with tin foil to prevent the extra hot steam from having direct contact with the egg for a hard fully-cooked yolk leave uncovered.

6. Put ramekins in the steamer basket and lower into pressure cooker. Close and lock the Lid in place. Set the pressure level to Low pressure.

7. Then, turn the heat up high and when the pan reaches pressure, lower the heat and count about 4 minutes cooking time at Low pressure.

8. When the timer beeps, do a quick pressure release. Remove the ramekins carefully.

9. Serve immediately and enjoy.

Bacon and Egg Risotto

Cook time: 10 minutes

Prep time: 10 minutes

Total time: 20 minutes

Serves: 2

Ingredients

- 3 slices of center cut bacon, chopped
- 1/3 cup chopped onion
- ¾ cup arborio rice
- 3 tbsp of dry white wine
- 1 ½ cups of chicken broth
- 2 eggs
- 2 tbsp of grated parmesan cheese
- salt and pepper, to taste
- chives, for garnish

Cooking Instructions

1. Select the sauté function on your pressure cooker and add the bacon.

2. Keep cooking until fat starts to render and bacon is crisping, about 5 minutes. Stir in the onion and cook 2 to 3 minutes more. Then, stir in the rice and sauté for 1 minute.

3. Pour in the wine and stir, scraping up any bits from the bottom of the pan.

4. When the wine has been absorbed, pour in the chicken broth and stir thoroughly. Then, close and lock the lid in place.

5. Ensure that the valve is in sealing position, then select the Manual function to cook on High Pressure for about 5 minutes.

6. When the rice has been brought to pressure, cook the eggs to your liking.

7. Once the rice is done cooking, do a quick pressure release and remove the Lid carefully.

8. Stir in the Parmesan, pepper and salt. Then, divide between two plates, add the cooked egg, and sprinkle with chives.

9. Serve immediately and enjoy.

Mexican Egg Casserole

Preparation time: 10 minutes

Cooking time: 25 minutes

Total time: 35 minutes

Serves: 7 to 8

Ingredients

- 8 large eggs, well-beaten
- 1 lb. of mild ground sausage
- ½ large red onion, chopped
- 1 red bell pepper, chopped
- 1 can of black beans, rinsed
- ½ cup green onions
- ½ cup flour
- 1 cup of cotija cheese
- 1 cup of mozzarella cheese
- Sour cream, cilantro to garnish (optional)

Cooking Instructions

1. Select the sauté function on your pressure cooker. Once it is hot, add the sausage and onion. Cook until the sausage is cooked through, for about 6-minutes.

2. Then, mix flour with eggs until well combined. Add the egg mixture to the sausage and onions in your pressure cooker.

3. Add the chopped vegetables, beans and cheeses. You can leave a little bit of the mozzarella cheese and put that on top of the casserole when it is done.

4. Close and lock the Lid in place. Set the pressure cooker to high pressure and allow to cook for 20 minutes.

5. When the pressure cooker beeps, allow the pressure to release naturally then remove the Lid carefully.

6. Take the casserole out of the pressure cooker. lift the inner pot out of the pressure cooker and then put a plate on top of the inner pot.

7. Then, flip it upside down so the casserole will pop out onto the plate. Then, Add the remaining cheese to the top of the casserole.

8. Let it sit for a couple of minutes until the cheese melts. Serve and enjoy.

Egg Bake

Serves 3 to 4

Ingredients

- Spray oil
- 6 eggs
- 2 cups of frozen hash browns
- ¼ cup of unsweetened almond milk
- ½ cup of fat free shredded cheddar cheese
- 1 tsp sea salt
- 1 teaspoon of pepper
- ½ onion, diced
- ½ green pepper, diced
- ½ red pepper, diced
- 1 cup of water
- Green onion garnish optional

Cooking Instructions

1. Spray oil on your Instant Pot liner and press the sauté button. Put onion, green pepper, and red pepper and stir until tender.

2. Press the cancel function on your Instant Pot, add frozen hash browns while Instant Pot is still warm. Keep stirring until hash browns become soft.

3. After stirring, spray oil on a heatproof bowl that will fit inside your Instant Pot liner without touching the edges.

4. Add onion, pepper, and hash browns mixture into the heatproof bowl. Whisk the eggs, milk, ¼ cup of fat free shredded cheddar, salt, and pepper together.

5. Pour the egg mixture into the heatproof bowl, stir until everything is coated. Pour 1 cup of water into your Instant Pot liner.

6. Place your heatproof bowl on top of your Instant Pot steamer rack and place it inside your liner with the steamer rack handles.

7. Close and lock the Lid in place. set vent to sealing, and set the Instant pot to high pressure and allow to cook for 20 minutes.

8. When time is up, do a quick pressure release. After the pressure release loosen the edges of the egg bake with a butter knife.

9. Sprinkle the remaining cheese on top and add green onions as garnish if you desire.

10. Serve and enjoy.

Western Omelet Quiche

Servings: 4 to 5

Ingredients

- 6 large eggs (beaten)
- ½ cup half and half
- ⅛ tsp. Himalayan high mineral Salt
- 8 oz. Canadian bacon (diced)
- ¾ cup of red and green bell peppers (diced)
- 3 spring onions (thinly sliced, reserving tops for garnish)
- ¾ cup of cheddar cheese (shredded)
- ¼ cup of cheddar cheese (shredded, for garnish, optional)

Cooking Instructions

1. Place the steamer rack in the bottom of your Instant Pot and add 1½ cups of water. Butter or spray your souffle dish, and set aside.

2. Whisk together the eggs, milk, salt and pepper in a large mixing bowl.

3. Add your diced Canadian bacon, diced colored peppers, spring onion slices, and cheese to your prepared 1-quart soufflé dish and mix well to combine.

4. Pour egg mixture over to top of the meat and stir to combine properly. Loosely cover the souffle dish with aluminum foil.

5. Use the long-handled trivet to place the dish in the Instant Pot liner. Then, close and lock the Lid in place.

6. Select Manual, high pressure and set to cook for 30 minutes. When the time is up, allow it to count for about 10 minutes.

7. Press the Cancel function to turn off, then do a quick pressure release. Open the Lid carefully, then lift out the souffle dish and remove the foil.

8. Sprinkle the top of the western quiche with additional cheese if desired. It will melt nicely or you can boil until lightly browned. Garnish with chopped spring onion.

9. Serve and enjoy.

Cheesy Egg Bake

Preparation time: 5 minutes

Cooking time: 20 minutes

Total time: 25 minutes

serves: 3 to 4

Ingredients

- 6 slices bacon, chopped
- 2 cups of frozen hash browns
- 6 eggs
- ¼ cup of milk
- ½ cup of shredded cheddar cheese
- 1 tsp. of kosher salt
- ½ tsp. of pepper
- optional add-ins: onion, red pepper, spinach, mushrooms, green onions

Cooking Instructions

1. Chop up the bacon into small pieces then sauté in your pressure cooker until crispy. Put any extra veggies that you desire and sauté until tender, for about 3 minutes.

2. Put the frozen hash browns and stir until slightly thawed, for about 2 minutes. Grease a heat proof container that will fit into your Pressure Cooker.

3. In a separate bowl, whisk the eggs, milk, shredded cheese, salt and pepper together and then add bacon and veggie mixture to the eggs.

4. Pour the egg mixture into your greased, heat proof container. Then pour in 1 ½ cups of water into your pressure cooker and set the steamer rack inside.

5. Place heat proof bowl with egg mixture on top of steamer rack. Close and lock Lid in place, select Manual high pressure and set to cook for 20 minutes.

6. When the time is up, do a quick pressure release. Loosen the edges then transfer to a large plate.

7. Serve with green onions and extra shredded cheese and enjoy.

Spanish Tortilla Potato Egg Frittata, Quiche

Preparation time: 10 minutes

Cooking time: 18 minutes

Total time: 28 minutes

Serves: 4 to 5

Ingredients

- 6 large eggs
- 4 ounces of French Fries (defrosted) (or Hash Browns or Raw Potatoes)
- 1 tbsp. of Butter melted
- ¼ cup of spanish onions, scallions or onions, diced
- ½ tsp. of sea salt, or to taste
- ¼ tsp. of freshly ground black pepper or to taste
- 1 tsp. of fox point seasoning or other seasoning
- 1 clove fresh garlic minced
- ¼ cup of milk
- 1 tsp. of tomato paste
- 4 ounces of Cheese grated
- 1.5 cups of water

Topping

- 1 oz. of cheese, If desired

Add in options

- Green bell pepper
- Bacon
- Spinach
- Ham
- Sausage

Cooking Instructions

1. Peel and slice the potatoes into thin strips and soak in water for about 20 minutes. In a medium bowl, whisk together eggs and seasonings until very frothy.

2. Then whisk the tomato paste and milk together in a mixing cup, after mixing add it to the egg mixture. Whisk the mixture well.

3. Put garlic and onion to the egg mixture. Grease casserole dish thoroughly. After greasing remove potatoes from water and dry with a paper towel.

4. Put the raw potatoes and pour in melted butter. Skip the melted butter if you are using defrosted French fries or hash browns.

5. Pour in egg mixture and any add ins and top with cheese if using you like. Add water to your Pressure Cooker and place a Steamer rack.

6. Place uncovered casserole dish on Steamer rack. Close and lock the Lid and ensure that the valve is on sealing position.

7. Select Manual function to cook on High-Pressure for about 15 to 20 minutes.

8. When the time is up, allow a 10-minutes natural pressure release and then release the remaining pressure.

9. Top with grated cheese if you like and place the Lid on top of your Pressure Cooker and allow cheese to melt.

10. Serve and enjoy.

Crustless Veggie Quiche

Preparation time: 10 minutes

Cooking time: 30 minutes

Total time: 40 minutes

Serves: 6 to 7

Ingredients

- 8 large eggs
- ½ cup of milk
- ½ cup of flour
- ¼ teaspoon of salt and ¼ teaspoon of pepper
- herbs (optional)
- 1 large red pepper, chopped
- 1 cup of tomatoes, sliced or chopped
- 2 large green onions, chopped
- 1 ½ cups of shredded cheese (you can use mozzarella,)
- any other veggies you want to add like peppers, zucchini, etc.

Cooking Instructions

1. Put steamer rack in the bottom of your Instant Pot. Make an aluminum foil sling and put it in the bottom of the Instant pot.

2. After putting the aluminum foil add 1 cup of water. Then whisk the eggs, milk, flour, salt and pepper together in a large bowl.

3. Put veggies and 1 cup of cheese until it's combined. Then, pour the mixture into a bowl that will fit inside the Instant Pot bowl.

4. Cover the bowl with aluminum foil and put the bowl on top of the Steamer rack inside your Instant Pot. Close and lock the Lid in place.

5. Select Manual function to cook on High-Pressure for about 30 minutes. When the time is up, allow the Instant Pot to release pressure naturally for about 10 minutes.

6. Open the Lid carefully and lift the bowl up using the sling then take off the aluminum foil.

7. Sprinkle the top of the quiche with the remaining ½ cup cheese, replace the aluminum foil and let sit until the cheese melts for about 3 minutes.

8. Serve and enjoy.

CHAPTER 4: POULTRY RECIPES

Thai Chicken Rice Bowl

Preparation time: 10 minutes

Cooking: time 10 minutes

Total time: 20 minutes

Servings: 3 to 4

Ingredients

- 2 tbsp. of olive oil
- 4 chicken breasts (about 2 pounds)
- 1 cup of uncooked long-grain white rice
- 2 cups of broth
- 1 tbsp. of peanut butter optional
- ½ cup of sweet chili Thai sauce
- 3 tbsp. of soy sauce - to taste
- ½ tbsp. of fish sauce
- ½ tbsp. of ginger minced
- ½ tbsp. of garlic minced
- 1 tsp. of lime juice
- 1 tsp. of Sriracha or hot sauce
- Cilantro optional garnish
- Shredded zucchini optional garnish
- Shredded carrots optional garnish
- Bean sprouts optional garnish
- Peanuts optional garnish

Cooking Instructions

1. Select the sauté function on your Instant Pot and add the olive oil.

2. Sear the chicken breasts for 2 to 3 minutes on either side to seal in their juices and transfer to a glass baking dish. Then turn off your instant pot.

3. In a medium bowl, Mix the sweet chili Thai sauce, ginger, soy sauce, fish sauce, ginger, lime juice, sriracha (and peanut butter if you like) together.

4. Pour the sauce over the chicken breasts and stir to combine properly. Then place the rice in the Instant Pot and add the chicken and sauce over the top.

5. Add the broth and close the Lid. Select Manual function to cook on High-Pressure for about 10 minutes.

6. When time is up, allow the Instant Pot to release pressure naturally.

7. Shred the chicken with two forks and then mix with the rice before serving.

8. Garnish with cilantro, shredded veggies and peanuts if you desire.

9. Serve with extra soy sauce to taste.

10. Enjoy.

Creamy Chicken Noodle Soup

Preparation time: 10 minutes

Cooking time: 10 minutes

Total time: 20 minutes

Serves: 3 to 4

Ingredients

- 3 large carrots peeled and sliced
- 2 stalks of celery sliced
- 1 cup of chopped spinach
- 1 boneless skinless chicken breast chopped (fresh or frozen)
- 1 tsp. of parsley
- 1 tsp. of salt
- ½ tsp. of thyme
- ¼ tsp. of garlic powder
- 1/8 tsp. of black pepper
- 4 cups of low sodium chicken broth
- 1 cup of short pasta such as Ditalini or Orzo
- 1 cup 1% milk
- 2 tbsp. of corn starch

Cooking Instructions

1. Add carrots, celery, spinach, chicken, parsley, thyme, salt, garlic powder, black pepper and chicken broth in your Instant Pot and stir well.

2. Close and lock the Lid in place and ensure that the valve is on sealing position. Select Manual function to cook on High-Pressure for about 4 to 5 minutes.

3. When the time is up, turn off the Instant Pot. Do a quick pressure release and open the lid carefully.

4. Select the sauté function on your Instant Pot and add the pasta. Cook and stir for 4 to 5 minutes until pasta is all dente.

5. Whisk the milk and corn starch together and stir into the soup. It will thicken immediately and continue to thicken as it sits and cools.

6. Serve and enjoy.

Buffalo Chicken Lettuce Wraps

Preparation time: 10 minutes

Cooking time: 15 minutes

Total time: 25 minutes

Serves: 3 to 4

Ingredients

- 1 large boneless skinless chicken breast (about 16-20 oz)
- 1 celery stalk (for cooking with the chicken)
- 1 medium onion, diced
- 1 clove of garlic
- 16 ounces of low sodium chicken broth
- ½ cup of buffalo wing sauce (about 6 oz)
- large lettuce leaves (Romaine or Iceberg)
- ½ cup shredded carrots
- 1 large celery stalk, thinly sliced (for topping the lettuce wraps)
- ranch dressing, for topping

Cooking Instructions

1. Put the chicken, onions, garlic, one celery stalk, buffalo wing sauce and broth to your Instant Pot.

2. Close and lock the Lid into place, and ensure that the valve is on sealing position.

3. Select manual setting and set the timer to cook for 15 minutes.

4. When the time is up, allow the Instant Pot to release pressure naturally for about 5 minutes. Then, do a quick pressure release to release the remaining pressure.

5. Shred the chicken with two forks and serve in lettuce cups topped with buffalo chicken, chopped celery, shredded carrots, and ranch.

6. Serve and enjoy.

Chipotle Chicken Black Beans and Rice

Preparation time: 10 minutes

Cooking time: 6 minutes

Total time: 16 minutes

Serves: 5 to 6

Ingredients

- 1 lb. of Boneless Skinless Chicken Breasts or thighs, cut into bite sized pieces
- 1 small onion chopped
- 4 cups of diced tomatoes in juice
- 1 tablespoon of chipotle peppers in adobo pureed
- ½ cup of filtered water
- 1 cup of jasmine rice uncooked
- ½ lime, juiced
- 2 teaspoon of sea salt (real salt)
- ½ teaspoon of finely ground black pepper
- 2tabspoon of butter (pasture raised, grass fed) ghee or coconut oil
- 1 can organic black beans drained & rinsed

Cooking Instructions

1. Combine chicken, onion, tomatoes with juice, peppers, water, lime juice, rice, salt, pepper and butter in your pressure cooker.

2. Cook under pressure for 6 minutes. When time is up, do a quick pressure release.

3. After the pressure release, open and add black beans then stir to combine.

4. Season with additional salt & pepper, to taste.

5. Serve with a garnish of shredded cheese, sour cream and guacamole for a complete meal.

6. Enjoy.

Chicken Breasts

Preparation time: 3 minutes

Cooking time: 20 minutes

Total time: 23 minutes

Serves: 3 to 4

Ingredients

- 1 tbsp. of oil (we use avocado, but you can use coconut or canola - something with a high smoke point is best)
- 3 boneless, skinless chicken breasts (uncooked)
- ¼ tsp. of garlic salt per chicken breast (you can use just garlic powder and regular salt)
- dash black pepper
- 1/8 tsp. of dried oregano
- 1/8 tsp. of dried basil
- 1 cup of water

Cooking Instructions

1. Preheat the sauté function on the Instant Pot at the highest setting. Add oil to the pot. Season one side of the chicken breasts.

2. After the display reads "hot," add the chicken breasts, seasoned side down, to the pot.

3. We used tongs to avoid hot oil splatter, add seasoning on the second side and cook for about 3 to 4 minutes on each side.

4. Remove it from pot with the tongs. Then add 1 cup of water to the pot (may need more for 8-quart pots), plus the steamer rack.

5. Place the chicken on the steamer rack. Close and lock the Lid in place, Select Manual function to cook on High-Pressure for about 5 minutes.

6. When time is up, allow the Instant pot to release pressure naturally for about 5 minutes. Then do a quick pressure release.

7. Remove the chicken from the pot, and allow to rest for about 5 minutes before serving.

8. Serve and enjoy.

Pulled Tandoori Chicken

Preparation time: 10 minutes

Cooking time: 35 minutes

Total time: 45 minutes

Serves: 4 to 5

Ingredients

- 2 to 3 large boneless, skinless chicken breasts
- ½ cup of water
- 3 cloves of garlic, minced
- 1 tbsp. of extra virgin olive oil or coconut oil
- ½ onion, minced
- 1 can of full fat coconut milk
- 2 teaspoons of smoked paprika
- 1 teaspoon of turmeric
- 1 ½ teaspoons of ground cumin
- 1 ½ teaspoons of black pepper
- 1 teaspoon of cayenne pepper - optional
- 2 tablespoons of cilantro for garnish
- 1 ½ teaspoons of sea salt, or to taste

Cooking Instructions

1. Place frozen chicken breasts in the Instant Pot with ½ cup of water. Close and lock the Lid in place and ensure that the valve is on sealing position.

2. Select Manual function to cook on High-Pressure for about 26 minutes. Using thawed chicken breasts, add ½ cup of water to your Instant pot.

3. Close and lock the Lid in place and ensure that the valve is on sealing position. Select Manual function to cook on High-Pressure for about 15 minutes.

4. When the time is up, do a quick release. Drain the water and remove the chicken. On a cutting board, spend a few minutes pulling the chicken.

5. Add the oil, garlic and onion to the Instant Pot. Select the sauté function on your Instant Pot and cook the onion and garlic 2 to 3 minutes.

6. Turn the sauté function off. Add the chicken back to the pot along with the coconut milk, cumin, turmeric, smoked paprika, and black pepper.

7. Stir to combine well. Add 1 ½ teaspoons of sea salt and stir to combine, add more as needed.

8. Serve immediately over rice and enjoy.

Cashew Butter Chicken

Preparation time: 5 minutes

Cooking time: 4 hours

Total time: 4 hours 5 minutes

Serves: 5 to 6

Ingredients

- 2 pounds of chicken breast large or chicken tenders
- ½ cup of smooth cashew butter
- ¼ cup of coconut aminos or GF Tamari Soy Sauce
- ¼ cup of honey
- ¼ cup of rice vinegar
- 1 tablespoon of sriracha
- ½ cup of chicken broth
- 3 cloves of garlic minced
- 1/3 cup of full fat canned coconut milk optional
- 3 tablespoons of chopped cilantro optional
- 3 tablespoons of chopped cashews optional

Cooking Instructions

1. Cut your chicken into small chunks, and place inside your Instant pot.

2. Mix cashew butter, coconut aminos or soy sauce, honey, rice vinegar, sriracha, chicken broth, and garlic together in a small bowl. Mix well to form a sauce and pour on top of the chicken.

3. Close and lock the Lid in place, Select Manual function to cook on High-Pressure for about 7 minutes.

4. When the timer beeps, do a quick pressure release to release the remaining pressure.

5. Shred the chicken or keep it in chunks. Stir in coconut milk (if using).

6. Serve over rice, cauliflower rice, or quinoa. Top with cashews and cilantro for garnish (if using).

7. Serve and enjoy.

Lemon Garlic Chicken

Ingredients

- 1 to 2 lb. of chicken breasts or thighs
- 1 tsp. of sea salt
- 1 onion, diced
- 1 tbsp. of avocado oil, lard, or ghee
- 5 garlic cloves, minced
- ½ cup of organic chicken broth or homemade
- 1 tsp. of dried parsley
- ¼ tsp. of aprika (omit for AIP)
- ¼ cup of white cooking wine (omit for AIP)
- 1 large lemon juiced (or more to taste)
- 3 to 4 tsp. (or more) arrowroot flour

Cooking Instructions

1. Select the sauté function on your Instant Pot and add the diced onion and cooking fat.

2. Cook the onions for 5 to 10 minutes or until (softened or start to brown).

3. Add in the remaining ingredients except for the arrowroot flour. Then close and lock the Lid in place.

4. Select Manual function to cook on High-Pressure for about 12 to 15 minutes and ensure that the valve is on sealing position.

5. When the time is up, release steam valve to vent and then carefully remove lid.

6. You may thicken your sauce by making a slurry.

7. To do this remove about ¼ cup of sauce from the pot, add in the arrowroot flour, and then reintroduce the slurry into the remaining liquid.

8. Stir and serve immediately.

Honey Curry Chicken

Preparation time: 5 minutes

Serves: 4 to 5

Ingredients:

- ¼ cup of unsalted butter, melted
- ½ cup of honey
- ¼ cup of yellow mustard
- 1 tsp. of salt
- 1 ½ tsp. of hot curry powder
- ¼ tsp. of cayenne pepper (adjust to taste)
- 1.5 pounds of boneless skinless chicken thighs or breasts

Cooking Instructions

1. Add butter, honey, mustard, salt, curry powder, and cayenne pepper to the pot of the pressure cooker and stir to combine well.

2. Add steamer rack to the pot and arrange chicken on steamer rack.

3. Select Manual function to cook on High-Pressure for (13 minutes for thighs or 18 minutes for breasts).

4. When the time is up, allow the pressure cooker to release pressure naturally for about 10 minutes. (Note: do not add any broth or water because the chicken itself contributes so much liquid as it cooks.)

5. When chicken is cooked, use two forks to transfer it to a serving dish.

6. Pull the chicken apart into pieces, cover with foil to keep warm while you finish the sauce.

7. Remove steamer rack from cooking pot and turn on sauté function.

8. Bring to gentle boil, stirring frequently to reduce and thicken sauce, about 5 minutes.

9. Add sauce to chicken and stir to coat.

10. Serve over steamed rice and enjoy.

Italian Chicken

Serves: 6 to 7

Ingredients

- 1 tbsp. of olive oil
- ¾ cup of onion
- ½ cup green bell pepper
- ½ cup of red bell pepper
- ¼ teaspoon of salt
- ¾ cup of marinara
- 2 tablespoons of pesto
- 2 pounds of chicken breasts
- ¾ cup of very thinly sliced mushrooms

Cooking Instructions

1. Select the sauté function on your Instant Pot and add the olive oil, onion, bell peppers and salt.

2. Sauté for 3 to 4 minutes or until the vegetables are softened, then add the marinara, pesto and chicken.

3. Cook thawed chicken on high pressure for 12 minutes. (Cook frozen chicken on high pressure for 20 minutes.)

4. When the time is up, do a quick pressure release.

5. Remove the chicken breasts from the pot and place on a cutting board. Use two forks to shred the chicken.

6. After shredding the chicken, remove ⅔ cup of liquid from the pot carefully to leave the vegetables. Reserve the liquid for cooking rice or making soup.

7. Add the mushrooms to the vegetables and sauté for 2 to 3 minutes until mushrooms are slightly softened.

8. Return the shredded chicken to pot and stir until well combined.

9. Serve and enjoy.

CHAPTER 5: FISH & SEAFOODS

Creamy Fish Chowder

Serves: 4 to 5

Ingredients

- ¾ cup of chopped bacon
- 1 small/medium onion, chopped
- 2 ribs celery, chopped
- 1 medium carrot, chopped
- 2 cloves of garlic, minced or pressed
- 3 cups of Peeled & Cubed Potatoes preferably Yukon gold
- 4 cups of chicken bone-broth or vegetable broth
- 2 tbsp. of butter (pasture raised, grass fed) or ghee
- 1 lb. of wild caught Haddock FiletsFROZEN
- 1 cup of frozen or freeze-dried corn
- sea salt (real salt)
- Ground White Pepper
- 2 cups of heavy cream
- 1 heaping tbsp. of organic potato starch

Cooking Instructions

1. Select the sauté function on your pressure cooker, cook bacon in butter until crispy.

2. Add onion, garlic, carrot and celery, cook for about 3 minutes. Season with sea salt and white pepper.

3. Add potatoes, corn, fish and broth. Cook under high pressure for 5 minutes.

4. When time is up, allow pressure cooker to release pressure naturally.

5. Combine heavy cream and potato starch, mix well. Add to chowder and Stir well.

6. Select the pressure cooker Warm function if it did not by default.

7. On the warm function, allow it to thicken slightly for about 2 to3 minutes.

8. Serve and Enjoy.

Shrimp and Lentil Stew

Preparation time: 10 Minutes

Cooking time: 12 Minutes

Total time: 22 minutes

Serves: 5 to 6

Ingredients

- 1 tbsp. of olive oil
- 3 cloves of garlic, minced
- 1 Onion, chopped small
- 1 red bell pepper, chopped
- 1 tbsp. of thyme
- 2 tsp. of oregano
- 2 tsp. of old Bay Seasoning
- ½ tsp. of Cayenne
- 1 cup of lentils
- 1 pound of shrimp, deveined and peeled
- 3 cups of chicken broth (or vegetable)
- 1 15 oz. can Diced Tomatoes, drain slightly
- ½ cup of tomato sauce
- 2 tbsp. of Worcestershire sauce
- 1 cup of frozen riced broccoli

Cooking Instructions

1. Select the sauté function on your Instant Pot and add the olive oil, garlic, onion, and bell pepper and sauté for 5 minutes.

2. Add the thyme, oregano, old bay, and cayenne and toss to mix, continue to sauté for an additional 1 minute.

3. Place the lentils, shrimp, chicken broth, diced tomatoes, tomato sauce, Worcestershire sauce and riced broccoli into your Instant Pot.

4. Select Manual function to cook on High-Pressure for about 12 minutes.

5. Release the steam and season with Salt and Pepper.

6. Serve and enjoy.

Coconut Red Curry Shrimp

Preparation time: 5 minutes

Cooking time: 25 minutes

Total time: 30 minutes

Serves: 5 to 6

Ingredients

- ¼ cup of coconut milk canned
- 1 teaspoon of cumin
- 1 teaspoon of paprika
- 2 teaspoons of curry spice
- 3 tablespoons of fresh lime juice
- ½ teaspoon of sea salt
- 1 teaspoon of freshly grated ginger
- 1 clove of garlic minced
- 2 pounds of large shrimp peeled and deveined

For Sauce

- 2 tablespoons of coconut oil or olive oil
- 1 small white onion diced
- 2 teaspoons of freshly grated ginger
- 2 cloves of garlic minced
- 1 28 oz. can of diced tomatoes
- 3 tablespoons of red Thai curry paste
- 1 14 oz. of coconut milk
- 1 teaspoon of sea salt
- 1/3 cup of freshly chopped cilantro for garnish optional

Cooking Instructions

1. Start by making your marinade. In a medium bowl, whisk coconut milk, spices, lime juice, sea salt, ginger, and garlic together. then add shrimp.

2. Toss to coat and let sit while you are preparing the sauce. Select the sauté function on your Instant Pot, once hot then add oil to coat the bottom of the pan.

3. After coating the bottom of the pan. Add onion, ginger, and garlic. Allow to Sauté for a few minutes, then select the cancel function.

4. Add tomatoes, curry paste, coconut milk, and salt. Close and lock the Lid in place and ensure that the valve is on sealing position.

5. Select the Manual function, and cook on High Pressure for about 7 minutes. When the time is up, do a quick pressure release on your Instant Pot.

6. Remove the lid carefully, and select cancel function on your Instant Pot. Select, sauté function and add in shrimp plus juices from the marinade.

7. Simmer until the shrimp is cooked through and no longer pink for about 4 to 5 minutes. Serve with optional cilantro, salt to taste, and over rice.

8. Serve and enjoy.

Fish Stew

Preparation time: 5 minutes

Cooking time: 15 minutes

Total time: 20 minutes

Serves: 3 to 4

Ingredients

- 4 tbsp. of extra-virgin olive oil, divided
- 1 medium red onion, quartered and thinly sliced
- 4 garlic cloves, roughly chopped
- ½ cup of dry white wine
- 8 ounces of bottle clam juice (or other seafood/shellfish stock)
- 2 ½ cups of water
- 1/2 pound of red or gold potatoes, diced
- 1 14 oz. of can diced tomatoes (or 1 1/2 cups diced fresh tomatoes), with their juices
- kosher salt and black pepper
- pinch of red pepper flakes, or to taste
- 1.5 to 2 pounds of boneless, skinless sea bass filets, cut into roughly 2" pieces
- 2 tbsp. of fresh lemon juice (from about 1 lemon)
- 2 tbsp. of chopped fresh dill

Cooking Instructions

1. Select the Sauté function on your Instant Pot to cook the onions in 2 tbsp. of olive oil, until browned and softened for about 3 minutes.

2. Add the garlic, and sauté until fragrant for about 30 seconds.

3. Add the white wine to deglaze. Scrap up any brown bits with a wooden spoon, until about half the wine has evaporated for about 1 minute.

4. Add the water, clam juice, potatoes, tomatoes, plenty of salt and pepper, and red pepper flakes. Turn the "sauté" function off.

5. Close and lock the Lid in place, then select the Manual function, and cook on High Pressure for about 5 minutes.

6. When the time is up, do a quick pressure release until the float valve is depressed.

7. Open your Instant Pot carefully and turn the Sauté function back on.

8. Once soup is simmering, add the fish pieces and simmer for 5 minutes, until fish is just cooked and flakes apart easily.

9. Turn off Sauté function, then stir in the lemon juice and fresh dill, along with the remaining 2 tbsp. of extra-virgin olive oil.

10. Taste and adjust seasoning if you desire.

11. Serve and enjoy.

Salmon

Preparation time: 10 minutes

Cooking time: 5 minutes

Total time: 15 minutes

Serves: 3 to 4

Ingredients

- 3 medium lemon
- ¾ cup of water
- 4 fillet salmon
- 1 bunch of dill weed, fresh
- 1 tbsp. of butter, unsalted
- ¼ tsp. of salt
- ¼ tsp of black pepper, ground

Optional

- 1 cup of brown rice, raw
- 4 cups of green beans

Cooking Instructions

1. Add ¼ cup of fresh lemon juice, and ¾ cup of water in the bottom of your Instant Pot.

2. Add the steamer rack.

3. Place the (Sockeye) salmon fillets, frozen, on top of the steamer rack.

4. Sprinkle fresh dill on top of the salmon, place one slice of fresh lemon on top of each one.

5. Close and lock the Lid in place, then select the Manual function, and cook on High Pressure for about 5 minutes.

6. When the time is up, select Cancel and do a quick pressure release.

7. Serve immediately with butter, extra dill and lemon, and salt and pepper.

8. Enjoy.

Shrimp

Ingredients

- 2 pounds of shrimp
- 2 tablespoons of oil
- 2 tablespoons of butter
- 1 tablespoon of garlic minced
- ½ cup of white wine
- ½ cup of chicken stock
- Pasta or cooked rice
- 1 tablespoon of lemon juice
- Parsley for garnish
- Salt & pepper to taste

Cooking Instructions

1. Add the oil and butter in your Instant Pot and select the Sauté function. When the butter is melted. Add in the garlic and cook until fragrant.

2. Then, add the white wine and chicken stock to deglaze the pot, and stir up any browned bits. Turn off the Sauté function and add the shrimp.

3. Then, close and lock the Lid in place. Select the meat/stew function, set to cook for 1 minute.

4. When time is up, allow the Instant Pot to release pressure naturally for about 5 minutes.

5. Open the Lid and stir in the cooked pasta or rice and add the lemon juice, salt and pepper to taste. Use 2 cups of rice and 3 cups of water to cook rice in your Instant Pot.

6. Use the rice button on your Instant Pot and allow to release pressure naturally for about 10 minutes.

7. Use 2 cups of pasta to 3 cups of water to cook pasta in your Instant Pot.

8. Use the soup button and cook for about 8 minutes, when time is up, do a quick pressure release.

9. Serve and enjoy.

Lemon Pepper Salmon

Preparation time: 5 minutes

Cooking time: 10 minutes

Total time: 15 minutes

Serves: 3 to 4

Ingredients

- ¾ cup of water
- A few sprigs of parsley dill, tarragon, basil or a combo
- 1 lb. of salmon filet skin on
- 3 tsp. of ghee or other healthy fat divided
- ¼ tsp. of salt or to taste
- ½ tsp. of pepper or to taste
- ½ lemon thinly sliced
- 1 zucchini julienned
- 1 red bell pepper julienned
- 1 carrot julienned

Cooking Instructions

1. Add water and herbs in your Instant Pot and then put in the Trivet, ensure that the handles are extended up.

2. Place salmon, skin down on rack. Then, drizzle salmon with ghee/fat, season with salt and pepper, and cover with lemon slices.

3. Close and lock the Lid in place and ensure that the valve is on sealing position.

4. Select the Steam function to cook for about 3 minutes. While salmon cooks, julienne your veggies.

5. When the time is up, do a quick pressure release. Select the Warm/Cancel button.

6. Remove lid carefully, then remove the rack with salmon and set on a plate. Remove the herbs and discard, add veggies. Then close and lock the Lid in place.

7. Select the Sauté function and allow the veggies cook for about 1 or 2 minutes.

8. Serve veggies with salmon and add remaining tsp. of fat to the pot and pour a little of the sauce over them if you like.

9. Serve and enjoy.

Drunken Clams

Preparation time: 10 minutes

Cooking time: 4 minutes

Total time: 14 minutes

Serves: 4 to 5

Ingredients

- ¼ cup (60 ml) olive oil
- 2 cloves of garlic, peeled and minced
- ¼ cup of finely chopped fresh basil
- 2 cups of (500 ml) pale ale
- 1 cup of (250 ml) water
- ½ cup of (125 ml) chicken broth
- ¼ cup of (60 ml) dry white wine
- 3 pounds of (1.44 kg) fresh clams, scrabbled
- 2 tablespoons freshly squeezed lemon juice

Cooking Instructions

1. heat olive oil in your Pressure Cooker over medium heat.

2. Add minced garlic and cook, stirring, until fragrant, for 2 minutes. Then stir in chopped fresh basil.

3. Add in water, beer, chicken broth, wine and lemon juice. Increase heat to high and bring mixture to a boil.

4. Boil for about 1 minute, after boiling arrange a steamer rack and steamer basket in your Pressure Cooker. Place clams in basket, then close and lock the Lid in place.

5. Set the burner heat to High Pressure, when the pressure cooker reaches High Pressure, reduce the burner heat to low.

6. Set timer to cook for about 4 minutes. When the time is up, carefully open the Lid.

7. Discard any clams that have not opened. Transfer the cooked clams to a serving bowl using a tong.

8. Pour cooking liquid over. Serve and enjoy.

Mussels

Serves: 3 to 4

Ingredients

- 2 tbsp. of butter
- 2 shallots chopped
- 4 garlic cloves minced
- ½ cup of broth
- ½ cup of white wine
- 2 pounds of mussels cleaned
- Lemon optional for serving
- Parsley optional for serving

Cooking Instructions

1. Clean and remove beards from mussels.

2. Discard any mussels that do not close when tapped against a hard surface or have cracks.

3. Place the chopped onions and butter in your Instant Pot, select Sauté function. Stir and sauté onions until translucent.

4. Add garlic and cook for 1 minute before adding broth and wine. Then turn off the sauté setting and carefully add the mussels to your Instant Pot.

5. Select the Manual function, and cook on High Pressure for about 5 minutes.

6. When time is up. Allow the Instant pot to release pressure naturally.

7. Serve with a squeeze of lemon juice (if you like) and a sprinkle of parsley.

8. Serve and enjoy.

Shrimp Paella

Preparation time: 10 minutes

Cooking time: 5 minutes

Total time: 15 minutes

Serves: 3 to 4

Ingredients

- 1 pound of jumbo shrimp, shell and tail on frozen
- 1 cup of Jasmine rice
- 4 tablespoons of butter
- 1 onion chopped
- 4 cloves of garlic chopped
- 1 red pepper chopped
- 1 cup of chicken broth
- ½ cup of white wine
- 1 teaspoon of paprika
- 1 teaspoon of turmeric
- ½ teaspoon of salt
- ¼ teaspoon of black pepper
- 1 pinch of saffron threads
- ¼ teaspoon of red pepper flakes
- ¼ cup of cilantro optional

Cooking Instructions

1. Select the Sauté function on your Instant Pot. Then add butter to your Instant Pot and melt.

2. Add onions and cook until softened. After cooking onions add garlic and cook for about 1 minute more.

3. Add in paprika, turmeric, salt, black pepper, red pepper flakes, and saffron threads to your Instant pot. Stir well and cook for 1 minute.

4. Add red peppers, rice and stir thoroughly. Then cook for about 30 seconds to 1 minute.

5. Add in chicken broth and white wine, ensure that all rice is covered. Add shrimp on top.

6. Turn off your Instant Pot. Close and lock the Lid in place, ensure that the valve is on sealing position.

7. Select the Manual function, and cook on High Pressure for about 5 minutes.

8. When the time is up, do a quick pressure release. Remove shrimp from pot and peel if desired.

9. Serve with Cilantro and enjoy.

Spicy Pineapple Shrimp

Preparation time: 10 minutes

Cooking time 2: minutes

Total time: 12 minutes

Serves: 3 to 4

Ingredients

- 1 large red bell pepper cleaned and sliced
- 12 oz. Calrose cice or quinoa
- ¾ cup of unsweetened pineapple juice
- ¼ cup of dry white wine
- 2 tbsp. of soy sauce
- 2 tbsp. of Thai sweet chili sauce
- 1 tbsp. of sambal oelek ground chili paste
- 1 lb. of Large Shrimp, tails on frozen
- 4 Scallions chopped, white and greens separated
- 1.5 cups of unsweetened pineapple chunks drained

Cooking Instructions

1. Drain Juice from Pineapple and reserve Pineapple Chunks aside.

2. Measure out ¾ cup of Pineapple Juice, then add Red Bell Peppers, Pineapple Juice, Wine, Chili Sauce, Soy Sauce, Sambal Oelek, Rice and chopped Scallions (the white part) to your Pressure Cooker.

3. Place frozen Shrimp on top, then secure the Lid ensuring that the valve is on sealing position.

4. Select Manual function, and cook on High Pressure for 2 minutes.

5. When the time is up, allow the Pressure cooker to release pressure naturally for about 10 minutes.

6. Add Pineapple Chunks and Scallion Greens and mix thoroughly.

7. Serve and enjoy.

Savory Shrimp with Tomatoes and Feta

Preparation time: 10 minutes

Cooking time: 12 minutes

Total time: 22 minutes

Serves: 5 to 6

Ingredients

Cook together

- 2 tbsp. of Butter
- 1 tbsp. of garlic
- ½ tsp. of red pepper flakes adjust to taste
- 1.5 cups of chopped onion
- 1 14.5 ounces of can tomatoes
- 1 tsp. of oregano
- 1 tsp. of salt
- 1 lb. of frozen shrimp 21 to 25 count, shelled

Add after cooking

- 1 cup of crumbled feta cheese
- ½ cup of sliced black olives
- ¼ cup of parsley

Cooking Instructions

1. Select the Sauté function on your Instant Pot.

2. Once it is hot, add the butter. Allow it to melt a little, then add garlic and red pepper flakes.

3. Add in onions, tomatoes, oregano and salt. Then pour in the frozen shrimp.

4. Set the Instant pot to LOW pressure 1 minute. When the time is up, do a quick pressure release.

5. Mix in the shrimp with the rest of the lovely tomato broth. Allow it to cool slightly. Right before serving.

6. Sprinkle the feta cheese, olives, and parsley if you desire.

7. Serve immediately and enjoy.

Creamy Chipotle Shrimp Soup

Preparation time: 5 minutes

Cooking time: 25 minutes

Total time: 30 minutes

Serves: 4 to 5

Ingredients

- 3 slices bacon, chopped
- 1 cup of onion, diced
- ¾ cup of celery, chopped
- 1 teaspoon of garlic
- 1 tablespoon of flour
- ¼ cup of dry white wine
- 1 ½ cups of chicken or vegetable broth
- ½ cup of whole milk
- 1 ½ cups of potatoes, cut into small (1/3-inch) cubes
- 1 cup of frozen corn kernels
- 2 teaspoons of diced canned chipotle peppers in adobo sauce
- ¾ teaspoon of salt
- ½ teaspoon ground black pepper
- ½ teaspoon of dried thyme
- ½ pound of shrimp, peeled and deveined
- ¼ cup of heavy cream

Cooking Instructions

1. Set your Instant Pot to Sauté function.

2. Add bacon to inner pot of Instant Pot and Sauté until crisp, for about 3 minutes, stirring frequently.

3. Then add in onions, celery and garlic. Sauté till vegetables have softened, for about 2 to 3 minutes.

4. Stir in flour and allow to cook for 30 seconds to 1 minute, Select Cancel function and add white wine to deglaze the pot.

5. Stir to remove brown bits from the bottom of your Pot. If not completely deglazed, add 1 or 2 tablespoons of broth.

6. Stir in broth, milk, potatoes, corn, Chipotle, salt, black pepper and thyme.

7. Secure the lid and select the Manual function, and cook on High Pressure for 1 minute.

8. When the time is up, do a quick pressure release. Stir in shrimp and cream.

9. Close and lock the Lid in place, Allow the shrimp to cook in the residual heat for 10 minutes.

10. Garnish each serving with scallions, parsley and/or crumbled bacon.

11. Serve and enjoy.

CHAPTER 6: BEEF RECIPES

Homemade Hamburger

Preparation time: 6 minutes

Cooking time: 4 minutes

Total time 10 minutes

Serves: 5 to 6

Ingredients

- 1 lb. of ground beef
- 2 cups of beef broth
- 16 ounces of cheddar cheese
- 4 ounces of American cheese
- 1 tablespoon of onion powder
- 1 tablespoon of garlic powder
- 16 ounces of elbow macaroni
- 8 ounces of milk or heavy cream

Cooking Instructions

1. Sauté ground beef and seasonings until crumbled and meat changes pink color.

2. Pour in uncooked pasta and broth, select the Manual function, and cook on High Pressure for about 4 minutes.

3. Do a quick pressure release, add milk and Stir in both kinds of cheese slowly.

4. Serve and enjoy.

Cheesesteak Sloppy

Preparation time: 10 minutes

Cooking time: 10 minutes

Total time: 20 minutes

Serves: 5 to 6

Ingredients

- 1 ½ pounds of ground beef
- 1 tablespoon of butter
- 1 chopped green bell pepper
- 2 tablespoons of ketchup
- 1 tablespoon of Worcestershire sauce
- ¼ cup of water
- 1 package Lipton Onion Soup Mix
- 8 ounces of provolone chopped
- Hamburger buns or sub rolls.

Cooking Instructions

1. Select the Sauté function on your Instant Pot.

2. Add butter, bell pepper and ground beef. Cook until the ground beef changes its pink color.

3. Add ketchup, Worcestershire sauce, water, and Lipton onion soup mix.

4. Select the Manual function, and cook on High Pressure for about 6 minutes.

5. When the timer beeps, add in cheese and mix until melted.

6. Serve with your favorite cheesesteak toppings on a hamburger.

7. Serve and enjoy.

Beef and Macaroni

Preparation time: 10 minutes

Cooking time: 5 minutes

Total time: 15 minutes

Serves: 5 to 6

Ingredients

- 1 lb. of ground beef (or turkey (or turkey, chicken, Italian sausage, rabbit, bison)
- 1 lb. of cavatappi or other macaroni
- 1 tbsp. of extra virgin olive oil
- ½ onion diced well
- ½ green bell pepper diced (optional)
- 3 cloves fresh garlic minced fine
- 28 oz. of pureed tomatoes
- 15 oz. of tomato sauce
- 3 oz. of tomato paste
- 1 tbsp. of Worcestershire sauce (2 tbsp. if using turkey)
- 2 tsp. of dried basil
- 2 tsp. dried parsley flakes
- 2 tsp. of sea salt
- 1 tsp. of light brown sugar
- ¼ tsp. of crushed red pepper flakes
- ¼ tsp. of freshly ground black pepper
- ¼ cup of dry red wine a good Cabernet!
- 2.5 cups fresh water

Cooking Instructions

1. Select the Sauté function on your Pressure Cooker and allow it to heat. Then add in olive oil to your Pressure Cooker cooking pot.

2. Dump in the beef and break into pieces as you brown. When meat is partially brown, add in onions (and peppers, if using) and sauté until meat is mostly brown.

3. Add in garlic and Sauté for 1 minute more, drain excess grease, if needed. Add the rest of the ingredients.

4. Secure the lid and ensure that the valve is on sealing position. Select the Manual function, and cook on High pressure for about 5 minutes.

5. When the time is up, allow a 5 minutes natural pressure release, then do a quick pressure release. Top with freshly grated cheese.

6. Serve and enjoy.

Spaghetti

Preparation time: 10 minutes

Cooking time: 10 minutes

Total time: 20 minutes

Serves: 5 to 6

Ingredients

- 1 pound of ground beef or leave out if you wish
- ¼ cup onion diced
- 1 teaspoon of garlic minced
- 1 jar spaghetti sauce (24 oz)
- 2 cups of water
- 8 ounces spaghetti noodles
- 2 tablespoons of olive oil
- 1 teaspoon of salt optional, to taste

Cooking Instructions

1. Select the Sauté function on your Instant Pot.

2. Add in olive oil, onions, and garlic and cook until onions are softened a bit.

3. Add in ground beef and cook until the ground beef changes its pink color. Drain grease or leave in, your choice.

4. Set your Instant Pot to Manual, High Pressure. Then, add jar of spaghetti sauce, water, break the noodles.

5. Push noodles into liquid until they are covered. Remember Don't stir.

6. Close and lock the Lid, ensure that the valve is on sealing position.

7. Set to cook for 10 minutes. When the time is up, do a quick pressure release.

8. Then stir and serve. Enjoy.

Goulash

Preparation time: 10 minutes

Cooking time: 4 minutes

Total time: 14 minutes

Serves: 5 to 6

Ingredients

- 1 pound of ground beef
- 1 large onion
- 3 cloves of garlic
- 2 15- oz. cans tomato sauce
- 2 15- oz cans diced tomatoes
- 2 tablespoons of Italian seasoning
- 3 tablespoons of soy sauce
- 3 cups of elbow noodles
- 2 ½ cups of water
- 3 bay leaves
- salt and pepper to taste

Cooking Instructions

1. Select the Sauté function on your Instant Pot.

2. Once it is hot, add ground beef garlic, salt, pepper, and onion. Then cook until the meat changes color to brown.

3. Drain fat then add tomato sauce, diced tomatoes, Italian seasoning, soy sauce, water, noodles, and bay leaves.

4. Select the Manual function, and cook on High Pressure for about 4 minutes.

5. When the time is up, do a quick pressure release. Take out the bay leaves and give everything a good stir.

6. Then top with Parmesan Cheese and enjoy.

Stuffed Pepper Casserole

Preparation time: 10 minutes

Cooking time: 10 minutes

Total time: 20 minutes

Serves: 7 to 8

Ingredients

- 2 bell peppers diced
- 1 pound of ground beef
- ½ onion diced
- 1 can chiles diced, 4 ounces
- 2 cups of HemisFares spaghetti sauce
- 1 cup of diced tomatoes I prefer petite version, canned
- 1 ½ cups of white rice uncooked
- 2 cups of water or vegetable broth
- ½ teaspoon of chili powder or more
- 1 teaspoon seasoned salt or more, to taste
- 1 cup of mozzarella or parmesan cheese shredded
- 1 tablespoon of olive oil
- ½ teaspoon of minced garlic

Cooking Instructions

1. Add olive oil to your Instant pot. Select the Sauté function on your Instant Pot, normal or low and start to brown your ground beef.

2. When it is still slightly pink add in diced bell peppers and onion. Then continue to cook together until onions and peppers are soften and beef is browned.

3. Turn off your Instant Pot. Leave the ground beef on the bottom of your pot and pour in spaghetti sauce, diced tomatoes, spices, chiles, uncooked rice, and either water or vegetable broth on top. Remember don't stir

4. Secure the lid and ensure that the valve is on sealing position.

5. Select the Manual function, and cook on Low Pressure for about 10 minutes.

6. When the time is up, do a quick pressure release.

7. Stir and serve topped with mozzarella cheese. Enjoy.

Taco Meat

Serves: 2 to 3

Ingredients

- 2 lb. of ground beef
- 4 tbsp. of oil
- 2 red onions, diced
- 3 green bell peppers, diced
- 5 garlic cloves, minced
- 2 tsp. of chili powder
- 2 tsp. of oregano
- 1 tsp. of salt
- 1 tsp. of dried basil
- ½ tsp. of turmeric
- ½ tsp. of black pepper
- 1 tsp. of paprika
- 1 tsp. of cumin
- ½ tsp. of cayenne
- ½ tsp. of chipotle powder
- Cilantro, garnish

Cooking Instructions

1. Add all the ingredients to your Instant Pot except for the ground beef.
2. Select the Sauté function on your Instant Pot and stir-fry for 5 to 6 minutes.
3. Add the ground beef to the pot and cook until mostly brown.
4. Close the Lid and ensure that the valve is on sealing position.
5. Select the Manual function, and cook on High Pressure for about 10 minutes.
6. When the time is up, do a quick pressure release.
7. Garnish with cilantro and serve.
8. Enjoy.

Vegetable Beef Soup

Ingredients

- 2 pounds of lean ground beef
- 1 large onion, diced
- 2 teaspoons of garlic, minced
- 1 can (14.5 oz) stewed tomatoes, with liquid
- 3 cups of beef broth
- 4 carrots, sliced into round disks
- 3 stalks of celery, sliced or diced
- 3 to 4 medium-large potatoes, cut into bite-sized chunks
- 3 tablespoon of tomato paste
- ½ teaspoon of salt
- ½ teaspoon of pepper
- 2 teaspoon of dried parsley flakes
- ½ teaspoon of ground oregano

Cooking Instructions

1. Select the Sauté function on your Instant Pot. Then add ground beef, onion, and garlic and sauté until beef is cooked through.

2. Drain off as much of the oil as you can. After draining add can of stewed tomatoes with liquid, breaking up the tomatoes into small pieces.

3. Stir in beef broth, diced vegetables, tomato paste, and seasonings.

4. Secure the Lid and ensure that the valve is on sealing position.

5. Select the Manual function, and cook for about 4 minutes.

6. When the time is up, do a quick pressure release. remove the lid.

7. Serve and enjoy.

Sweet Potato Chili

Total time: 25 minutes

Preparation time: 5 minutes

Cooking time: 20 minutes

Ingredients

- 1 tsp. of olive oil
- 1 medium onion diced
- 3 garlic cloves minced
- ½ lb. of ground pork
- 1 lb. of ground beef
- 1 large sweet potato peeled and cut into 1/2-inch pieces
- 3 celery stalks sliced
- 3 ½ cups or 1 (28-ounce) can crushed tomatoes
- 1 tbsp. of Worcestershire sauce or coconut aminos
- 1 tsp. of cumin
- 1 tsp. of chili powder
- salt and pepper to taste

Optional toppings:

- diced avocado

Cooking Instructions

1. Select the Sauté function on your Instant.

2. Add in olive oil and diced onion to the interior pot. Sauté until tender and then add minced garlic, ground pork, and ground beef.

3. Cook, stirring frequently, until the pork and beef are browned. Add in sweet potato, celery, crushed tomatoes, Worcestershire sauce, cumin, and chili powder.

4. Give everything a good stir to combine well and situate the top onto the Instant Pot.

5. Select the Manual function, and cook on High Pressure for about 10 minutes.

6. When the time is up, Allow the Instant Pot to release pressure naturally and then carefully release the rest pressure before removing the Lid.

7. Serve the chili with any additional toppings desired. Enjoy.

Beef Stroganoff

Ingredients

- 2 tbsp. of olive oil
- ¾ pound of ground beef or turkey
- ½ cup of chopped red onion
- 1 tbsp. of garlic
- 4 oz. sliced Mushroom
- 2 10.5 oz. cans Campbell's condensed French onion soup
- 2 cups of water
- Salt to taste
- Pepper to taste
- 1 tbsp. of cornstarch)
- ¾ bag of egg noodles
- ½ cup of Greek yogurt or sour cream

Cooking Instructions

1. Spray Instant Pot interior with cooking spray. Select the Sauté function on your Instant Pot to sauté.

2. Drizzle 1 tbsp. cooking oil (we used olive) and brown ground beef or turkey, onion, and garlic.

3. Drain excess grease and return to pot. Then add mushrooms and sauté for another 1 or 2 minutes.

4. Add water, onion soup, salt, pepper and mix well. Whisk in cornstarch, add noodles.

5. Secure the Lid. Select the Manual function, and cook on High Pressure for about 6 minutes.

6. When the time is up, allow the pressure to release naturally for about 5 minutes, and then do a quick pressure release.

7. Stir in Greek Yogurt until combined.

8. Serve and enjoy.

Bolognese

Total time: 60 minutes

Preparation time: 15 minutes

Cooking time: 45 minutes

Ingredients:

- 4 oz. of pancetta (or center cut bacon), chopped
- 1 tbsp. of unsalted butter
- 1 large white onion, minced
- 2 celery stalks (about 3/4 cup), minced
- 2 carrots (about 3/4 cup), minced
- 2 pounds of lean ground beef
- ¼ cup of dry white wine, such as Pinot Grigio
- 2 (28 ounces) cans crushed tomatoes (I love Tuttorosso)
- 3 bay leaves
- ½ tsp. of kosher salt and fresh black pepper, to taste
- ½ cup half & half cream
- ¼ cup chopped fresh parsley

Cooking Instructions

1. Select the Sauté function on your Instant Pot, Sauté the pancetta over low heat until the fat melts, for about 4 to 5 minutes.

2. Add in the butter, onion, celery and carrots and cook until soft, for about 6 to 7 minutes. Add the meat and season it with ¾ tsp. of salt and black pepper to taste.

3. Sauté until browned, for about 4 to 5 minutes, breaking the meat up into smaller sizes with a wooden spoon as it cooks.

4. Pour in the wine and cook until it reduces down, for about 3 to 4 minutes. Add crushed tomatoes, bay leaves, ¾ tsp. of salt and fresh cracked black pepper.

5. Secure the Lid, select the Manual function, and cook on High Pressure for about 15 minutes.

6. When the time is up, allow the pressure to release naturally, stir in the half & half and garnish with parsley.

7. Serve over your favorite pasta, zucchini noodles or spaghetti squash. Enjoy.

Picadillo

Preparation time: 5 minutes

Cooking time: 15 minutes

Total time: 20 minutes

Serves: 4 to 5

Ingredients

- 1 to 1 ½ pounds of lean ground beef
- 1 medium chopped onion
- 4 to 5 cloves garlic, minced
- 1 red bell pepper, finely chopped or, 1 pound of sweet mini peppers, diced
- 4 tbsp. of cilantro
- 1 tomato, finely chopped
- 1 teaspoon of ground cumin
- ½ teaspoon of paprika
- ½ teaspoon of garam marsala
- 1 teaspoon of salt
- ¼ teaspoon of black pepper
- 2 bay leaves
- 3 tbsp. of green olives or capers, finely chopped + juice
- 3 ounces tomato sauce
- 2 ounces of water

Cooking Instructions

1. Select the Sauté function on your Instant Pot, combine the meat and season with pepper, salt, garam marsala, paprika, chili powder and cumin.

2. Make use of your spoon to break up the meat into small sizes and sauté until the meat changes pink color.

3. Add in the onion, garlic, pepper, ½ of the cilantro, and tomato and sauté in with the beef approximately 2 to 3 minutes.

4. Add in the bay leaf, tomato sauce and water and mix well. Secure the Lid, ensure that the valve is on sealing position.

5. Select the Manual function, and cook on High Pressure for about 5 minutes. When the time is up, do a quick pressure release.

6. Stir in the remaining cilantro. Enjoy with rice.

Mongolian Beef

Preparation time: 3 minutes

Cooking time: 17 minutes

Total time: 20 minutes

Serves: 3 to 4

Ingredients

- 1 ½ pounds of Flank steak
- ¾ cup of soy sauce
- ½ cup of brown sugar
- ¼ cup of water
- ½ tsp. of fresh ginger minced
- 1 garlic clove minced
- 1 carrot shredded
- 1 tbsp. of olive oil
- 1 green onion sliced (garnish)

To thicken sauce

- 3 tbsp. of cornstarch
- 3 tbsp. of water

Cooking Instructions

1. In a medium bowl, slice flank steak into strips, combine soy sauce, water, oil, sugar, ginger, and garlic.

2. Add sauce in the instant pot, then add beef strips and shredded carrot. Mix until the beef is coated in the sauce.

3. Select the Manual function, and cook on High Pressure for about 8 minutes.

4. When the time is up, allow the pressure to release naturally for about 10 minutes before releasing the remaining pressure.

5. Combine the water and the cornstarch in a medium bowl until there are no lumps.

6. Select the Sauté function on your Instant Pot and pour in the cornstarch mixture. Allow the sauce to boil until it thickens for about 1 to 2 minutes.

7. Pour the beef into a platter and garnish with green onions. Serve and enjoy.

CHAPTER 7: PORK RECIPES

Ground Pork Casserole

Preparation time: 10 minutes

Cooking time: 20 minutes

Total time: 30 minutes

Serves: 5 to 6

Ingredients

- 1 pound of ground pork
- 2 cups of diced raw potatoes
- 1 ½ cups of sliced carrots
- 1 cup of chopped celery
- ½ cup of chopped onion
- 1 cup of frozen peas
- 1 cup of frozen whole kernel corn
- 1 10 ounces can tomato soup
- ½ cup of water
- 1 teaspoon of dried parsley flakes
- salt and pepper to taste

Cooking Instructions

1. Select the brown function on your Instant Pot, brown meat, onion, and celery. (If your device doesn't have a browning setting, you can use large skillet).

2. Combine meat mixture, potatoes, carrots, peas, and corn. Stir in tomato soup, water, parsley flakes, salt, and pepper, and give everything a good stir.

3. Secure the Lid and select the Manual function, to cook on High Pressure for about 20 minutes.

4. When the time is up, do a quick pressure release.

5. Serve and enjoy.

Pork Chops with Gravy

Preparation time: 5 minutes

Cooking time: 20 minutes

Total time: 25 minutes

Serves: 3 to 4

Ingredients

- 5 pork chops bone in or out
- 1 tbsp. of olive oil
- 1 tsp. of salt
- ½ tsp. of garlic powder
- ½ tsp. of pepper
- 1 envelope ranch dressing mix
- 1 one oz. envelope brown gravy mix
- 1 10.5 oz. can cream of chicken soup
- 2 cups of beef broth
- 2 tbsp. of cornstarch
- 2 tbsp. of water

Cooking Instructions

1. Season the pork chops on both sides with the salt, garlic powder, and pepper. Select the Sauté function on your Instant Pot and add in olive oil.

2. Once the oil is hot brown the pork chops on each side for 2 to 3 minutes just until browned. Remove the pork chops from your Instant Pot.

3. Pour in ¼ cup of the beef broth to your Instant Pot and use a wooden spoon to deglaze the bottom of the pot.

4. Turn off your Instant Pot, add the pork chops along with the ranch dressing mix, brown gravy mix, cream of chicken soup, and remaining beef broth to the pot.

5. Secure the Lid and ensure that the valve is on sealing position. Select Manual function, and cook for about 8 minutes.

6. When the time is up, allow to release pressure naturally for about 10 minutes. After natural pressure release, release the remaining pressure and remove the Lid.

7. Transfer the pork chops from the pot to a serving plate. Whisk together the cornstarch and water in a medium bowl.

8. Select the Sauté function on your Instant Pot and whisk in the cornstarch mixture. Whisk constantly until gravy is thick, then, turn off your instant pot.

9. Serve the pork chops with the gravy and your favorite side dishes.

10. Serve and enjoy.

Pulled Pork

Preparation time: 35 minutes

Cooking time: 45 minutes

Total time: 1 hr. 5 minutes

Serves: 8 to 9

Ingredients

- 4 pounds of boneless pork loin or boneless pork shoulder/butt
- 1 teaspoon of kosher salt
- ½ teaspoon of black pepper
- 1 to 2 chipotle peppers in adobo sauce, minced
- 12 ounces Dr pepper soda
- your favorite BBQ sauce

Cooking Instructions

1. Slice pork into 4 pieces and season with salt and pepper.

2. Place pork in your instant pot, insert and top with minced chipotle peppers.

3. Pour Dr pepper around the pork. Then secure the Lid and ensure that the valve is on sealing position.

4. Select the Manual function, and cook for about 45 minutes. When the time is up, allow to release pressure naturally for about 15 minutes.

5. After natural pressure release, do a quick pressure release to get rid of the remaining pressure.

6. Transfer the pork to a large mixing bowl (it will be so tender it may start to fall apart during the transfer).

7. Shred the pork with two forks and add bbq sauce to your tastes.

8. Serve and enjoy.

Pork Chili

Preparation time: 10 minutes

Cooking time: 30 minutes

Total time: 40 minutes

Serves: 6 to 7

Ingredients

- 2 tbsp. of olive oil
- ½ sweet onion, chopped
- 3 garlic cloves, minced
- 1 red bell pepper, diced {seeds removed}
- 2 tbsp. of tomato paste
- 1 tsp. of salt
- 1 lb. of ground pork
- 3 tbsp. of chili powder
- 2 tsp. of cumin
- 1 tsp. of paprika
- ¼ tsp. of coriander
- 1 tsp. of Mexican oregano {or regular oregano}
- 1 – 16 oz. can of black beans, drained and rinsed
- 1 – 16 oz. can of corn, drained and rinsed
- 1 – 16 oz. can of fire roasted diced tomatoes {or regular diced tomatoes}
- 2 – 6 oz. cans of diced chiles
- 2 cups of stock {you can use vegetable, chicken or beef}

Garnish

- Sour cream
- Cheese
- Cilantro
- Red Onion
- Jalapeno

Cooking Instructions

1. Select the Sauté function on your Instant Pot and add in 2 tbsp. of olive oil. Add the onion, bell peppers and garlic and sauté until tender, for about 3 to 4 minutes.

2. Add the tomato paste and sauté for 1 minute more. Then, add 1 tsp. of salt and the pork and continue to sauté until the pork is almost cooked through.

3. Add the spices and Sauté until the pork is cooked through and the spices are aromatic.

4. Add in all of the remaining ingredients and give everything a good stir to combine.

5. Secure the Lid, select Manual function, and cook on High Pressure for about 15 minutes.

6. When the time is up, do a quick pressure release. Adjust seasonings to your tastes and garnish with your favorite toppings

7. Serve immediately and enjoy.

Pork Green Chili

Serves: 7 to 8

Ingredients

- 3 lb. of pork shoulder, trimmed of excess fat and cut into 1-inch cubes
- Kosher salt and freshly ground black pepper
- 3 tbsp. of vegetable oil
- 2 lb. of tomatillos, peeled and quartered
- 3 poblano peppers, seeded and diced
- 3 jalapeno peppers, seeded and diced
- 1 yellow onion, diced
- 4 cloves of garlic, minced
- 1 tbsp. of ground cumin
- 4 cups of chicken broth
- 1 bunch fresh cilantro, chopped
- Tortilla chips, for serving
- Shredded Mexican cheese blend, for serving
- Diced red onion, for serving
- Diced avocado, for serving

Cooking Instructions

1. Select the Sauté function on your Instant Pot, While the pot is heating, season pork with salt and black pepper.

2. Once the bottom of the pot is hot, then add the oil and cook the pork shoulder in batches until browned on all sides, for about 5 to 10 minutes.

3. Transfer the pork to a plate. Repeat with remaining pork until all pork is browned.

4. Return pork to the pot and add in tomatillos, peppers, onion, garlic, cumin and chicken broth.

5. Secure the Lid, and select the Manual function, to cook for 30 minutes.

6. When the time is up, do a quick pressure release and open the lid carefully.

7. Stir in cilantro and season to taste with salt and pepper.

8. Serve with tortilla chips, cheese, red onion, and avocado.

9. Serve and enjoy.

Spicy Pork & Spinach Stew

Preparation time: 10 minutes

Cooking time: 30 minutes

Total time: 40 minutes

Serves: 3 to 4

Ingredients

- 1 large onion
- 4 cloves garlic
- 10 oz. of Rotel
- 1 tsp. of dried thyme
- 2 tsp. of tony chachere seasoning or other cajun seasoning blend
- 1 lb. of pork butt or beef meat cut into 2-inch chunks

For finishing

- ½ cup of heavy whipping cream
- 4 to 6 cups of chopped baby spinach

Cooking Instructions

1. Blend onion, garlic, and Rotel together. If you don't have Rotel, use 14 ounces can of tomatoes and 5 ounces can of green chilis (poblano-style).

2. Pour into your Instant Pot, then add the Tony chachere or other Cajun seasoning mix. Add in the pork/beef cubes and give everything a good stir.

3. Secure the Lid and ensure that the valve is on sealing position. Select the Meat function, and cook for about 20 minutes.

4. When the time is up, allow it to release pressure naturally for about 10 minutes and then get rid of the remaining pressure.

5. Select the Sauté function on your Instant Pot. When the stew starts to boil, add the cream and give everything a good stir.

6. Then, add the spinach leaves and cook until wilted.

7. Serve and enjoy.

Pork Stew with Fall Vegetables

Preparation time: 15 minutes

Total time: 50 minutes

Serves: 3 to 4

Ingredients

- 1 ½ pounds of pork shoulder cubes
- 3 tbsp. of olive oil
- 1 onion, chopped
- 1 red bell pepper, seeded and diced
- 2 cloves garlic, chopped
- 1 rutabaga, peeled and cubed
- 4 carrots, peeled and cut into large pieces
- 8 whole baby potatoes
- 1 can diced tomatoes
- ½ cup of chicken broth
- Salt and pepper

Cooking Instructions

1. In a large skillet over high heat, brown the pork in 2 tablespoons (30 ml) of the oil. season with salt and pepper. And reserve aside.

2. In a Pressure Cooker over medium heat, soften the onion, bell pepper and garlic in the remaining oil (1 tablespoon/15 ml).

3. Add in the pork, rutabaga, potatoes, carrots, tomatoes and broth. season with salt and pepper.

4. Secure the Lid, cook on High Pressure for about 20 minutes.

5. When the time is up, allow it to release pressure naturally.

6. Serve immediately and enjoy.

Pozole (Pork and Hominy Stew)

Total time: 1 hour

Preparation time: 10 minutes

Cooking time: 50 minutes

Ingredients

- 1 ¼ lb. od boneless pork shoulder, trimmed of fat and cut into 4-inch pieces
- Kosher salt and fresh cracked pepper
- 1 tablespoon of olive oil, divided
- 1 medium white onion, chopped
- 4 garlic cloves, minced
- 2 tbsp. of chili powder
- 4 cups of low sodium chicken broth
- 2 cups of water
- 2 (15 oz) cans hominy, drained and rinsed
- 4 ounces diced avocado and lime wedges, for serving
- cilantro for garnish

Cooking Instructions

1. Season the pork with salt, then select the Sauté function and heat half of the oil.

2. Add in the pork and cook until pieces are browned on all sides, for about 8 minutes. Remove it from your pot and transfer to a plate.

3. Add the remaining oil, onion, garlic, and chili powder and sauté until soft, for about 4 minutes.

4. Add the broth and water, then cook. Stir and scrap up the brown bits with a wooden spoon. Return pork to your Pressure Cooker. Close and lock the Lid in place.

5. Cook on high pressure until meat is tender, for about 45 minutes. When the time is up, do a quick pressure release.

6. Then remove lid carefully. Skim fat if any, use two forks to shred the pork.

7. Stir in hominy and heat through. Serve with avocado and lime and garnish with cilantro.

8. Serve and enjoy.

Coca-Cola Pulled Pork

Preparation time: 15 minutes

Cooking time: 1 hour 30 minutes

Total Time 1 hour 45 minutes

Serves: 7 to 8

Ingredients

- 2 tablespoons of olive oil
- 4 pounds of boneless pork shoulder
- 1 teaspoon of salt
- 1 teaspoon of pepper
- 1 teaspoon of garlic powder
- 1 teaspoon of onion powder
- 1 teaspoon of smoked paprika
- ¼ cup of brown sugar
- 16 oz. Coca-Cola
- 3 cloves garlic
- 1 ½ cups of bbq sauce divided

Cooking Instructions

1. Select the Sauté function on your Instant Pot Set. Then add in oil to Instant Pot and allow oil to get hot.

2. Use tongs to sear all sides of your pork shoulder. If it doesn't fit in one piece you can cut it into 4 smaller pieces.

3. In a small bowl, mix all dry spices and brown sugar. Sprinkle over all sides of the pork shoulder. Place pork shoulder in the Instant Pot.

4. Pour Coca-Cola in your Instant Pot. Add garlic cloves. Add half of the bbq sauce in Instant Pot. (If you want more liquid, you can add ¼ cup of chicken or vegetable broth).

5. Secure the Lid, select the Meat/Stew function, and cook for about 90 minutes. When the time is up, allow it to release pressure naturally.

6. Remove pork shoulder and place it on a cutting board. Pull the meat apart with two forks.

7. Select the Sauté function on your Instant Pot. Heat up sauce left inside and add the remaining half of your bbq sauce.

8. Heat thoroughly. (Add 1 teaspoon of corn starch to sauce if you would like a thicker sauce).

9. Add meat back into Your Instant Pot. Stir until sauce coats the meat perfectly.

10. You can leave in Instant Pot on keep warm or remove and place in a bowl.

11. Serve and enjoy.

CHAPTER 8: APPETIZERS

Salsa

Ingredients

- 12 cups of diced, peeled & seeded fresh tomatoes
- 2 medium green peppers chopped & diced
- 3 large yellow onions chopped & diced
- 1 cup of seeded & chopped jalapeno peppers (You can roast first for a milder flavor)
- 36 ounces cans of tomato paste
- ½ cup of vinegar
- 3 tablespoons of sugar
- 1 tablespoon of salt
- 2 tablespoons of garlic powder
- 3 tablespoons of cayenne pepper (use less for milder heat)
- 4 tablespoons of cilantro (optional)

Cooking Instructions

1. Combine all the ingredients in your Instant Pot.

2. Select the Manual function, cook on High Pressure for about 30 minutes.

3. When the time is up, allow it to release pressure naturally.

4. After natural pressure release, allow to cool and can or freeze in airtight containers.

5. Serve and enjoy.

Sweet and Spicy Meatballs

Preparation time: 5 minutes

Cooking time: 25 minutes

Total time: 30 minutes

Ingredients

- 16 ounces of cooked perfect meatballs
- 12 oz. of chili sauce
- 12 oz. of grape jelly
- ½ cup of water
- ½ tbsp. of crushed red pepper
- ½ tsp. of cayenne pepper

Garnish: chopped green onions (opt)

Cooking Instructions

1. Add 16 oz. of cooked perfect meatballs to the Instant Pot.

2. Combine chili sauce, grape jelly, water and spices in a medium bowl, give everything a good stir to combine.

3. Pour the mixture over cooked perfect meatballs and stir to cover. Secure the Lid, select the Manual function, to cook for about 10 minutes.

4. When the time is up, do a quick pressure release. Garnish with chopped green onions.

5. Serve and enjoy.

Hawaiian Meatballs

Serves: 3 to 4

Ingredients

- 1 package of cooked perfect sweet italian meatballs
- 1 can of pineapple chunks with juice
- 1 red pepper, chopped
- ¾ cup of brown sugar
- 1 tbsp. of soy sauce
- ¼ cup of red onion
- 1/3 cup of water

Cooking Instructions

1. Place all the ingredients (except for corn starch) in your Instant Pot and give everything a good stir.

2. Secure the Lid, select the Manual function, cook on High Pressure for about 5 minutes.

3. When the time is up, do a quick pressure release.

4. After the pressure release, select the Sauté function on your Instant Pot, whisk in 1 tbsp. of cornstarch until thickened.

5. Serve over rice and enjoy.

White Queso Dip

Preparation time: 10 minutes

Cooking time: 20 minutes

Total time: 30 minutes

Serves: 9 to 10

Ingredients

- ¾ pound of white American cheese slices
- 1 cup of queso shredded cheese mix
- 1 tbsp. of butter
- 18 ounces package cream cheese
- 1 tbsp. of garlic
- 1 can Rotel
- 1 tbsp. of milk
- 1 tsp. of oregano
- 1 cup of water

Cooking Instructions

1. Add one cup of water in the bottom of the Instant Pot.

2. Cover the bottom of the Instant Pot safe bowl with tin foil

3. Place on a steamer rack that has been placed on the bottom of the Instant Pot.

4. Add in all ingredients and cover the top of the bowl with tin foil.

5. Secure the Lid, select the Manual function, cook on High Pressure for about 18 minutes.

6. When the timer beeps, do a quick pressure release and remove Lid carefully.

7. Remove tin foil and whisk immediately until smooth.

8. Serve and enjoy.

Cheddar Bacon Ale Dip

Total time: 25 minutes

Preparation time: 15 minutes.

Cooking time: 10 minutes.

Ingredients

- 18 oz. cream cheese, softened
- ¼ cup of sour cream
- 1-1/2 tbsp. of Dijon mustard
- 1 tsp. of garlic powder
- 1 cup of beer or nonalcoholic beer
- 1 lb. of bacon strips, cooked and crumbled
- 2 cups of shredded cheddar cheese
- ¼ cup of heavy whipping cream
- 1 green onion, thinly sliced
- Soft pretzel bites

Cooking Instructions

1. In a Pressure Cooker, combine cream cheese, sour cream, mustard and garlic powder until smooth.

2. Stir in beer, add bacon, reserving 2 tbsp. Secure the Lid and ensure that the valve is on sealing position.

3. Select the Manual function, cook on High Pressure for about 5 minutes.

4. When the time is up, do a quick pressure release. Select the Sauté function, and adjust for normal heat.

5. Stir in cheese and heavy cream. Cook and stir until mixture has thickened, for about 3 to 4 minutes.

6. Transfer to serving dish. Sprinkle with onion and reserved bacon. Serve with pretzel bun bites.

7. Serve and enjoy.

Buffalo Chicken Dip

Preparation time: 5 minutes

Cooking time: 20 minutes

Total time: 25 minutes

Serves: 7 to 8

Ingredients

- ¾ cup of cottage cheese
- ¾ cup of plain Greek yogurt
- 2/3 shredded cheddar cheese
- 2 pounds of frozen chicken breasts
- ¾ cup of Frank's hot sauce
- ½ teaspoon of garlic powder
- ½ teaspoon of onion powder
- ¼ teaspoon of black pepper
- ½ teaspoon of dried dill
- ½ teaspoon of dried parsley
- ½ teaspoon of salt
- Goat or feta cheese crumbles garnish
- Green onions garnish

Cooking Instructions

1. Add in frozen chicken breast and 1 cup of water to your Instant Pot insert. Secure the Lid, ensure that the valve is on sealing position.

2. Select the Manual function, cook on High Pressure for about 12 minutes. When the time is up, allow it to release pressure naturally.

3. While the chicken is cooking prepare your sauce. In a blender mix together the cottage cheese, Greek yogurt, and seasoning (garlic powder, onion powder, pepper, salt, dill, and parsley) until smooth for 1 to 2 minutes.

4. When the chicken is done cooling, drain the liquid and shred the chicken in the Instant Pot using a hand mixer.

5. Select the Sauté function on your Instant Pot, mix in the cheese, buffalo sauce, and blended sauce.

6. When the cheese is melts, transfer the dip to an oven safe serving dish. Sprinkle with goat cheese if desired.

7. Place in the broiler until the top is golden, for about 5 minutes.

8. Remove from the oven and let the dip rest for 5 to 10 minutes. Top with green onions if you like.

9. Serve with celery, carrots, whole wheat cracker and enjoy.

Crispy Chicken Wings

Cooking time: 30 minutes

Total time: 30 minutes

Ingredients

- 2 pounds of chicken wingettes
- 2 cups of wing sauce
- 1 cup of water

For serving: ranch, blue cheese, celery, carrots

Cooking Instructions

1. Place the wings in the bottom of your Instant Pot, add in water and 1 cup of sauce.

2. Close and lock the Lid in place, select the Manual function, cook for about 10 minutes.

3. When the time is up, do a quick pressure release. While the wings are cooking, prepare a sheet pan with aluminum foil, then place a wire rack on top, and spray with cooking spray.

4. Preheat your oven to broil, with the rack, 6 inches from the top. Use tongs to remove the wings to the prepared pan.

5. Broil for 5 minutes, flip them and broil for another 5 minutes more. Baste them with remaining 1 cup of sauce and broil for 3 to 5 more minutes.

6. baste again, halfway through, flip and repeat on the other side.

7. Serve with ranch, blue cheese, celery and carrots.

8. Serve and enjoy.

Stuffed Peppers

Preparation time: 15 minutes

Cooking time: 10 minutes

Total time: 25 minutes

Serves: 7 to 8

Ingredients

- 8 bell peppers
- ½ pound of ground beef
- 2 cups of uncooked minute rice
- 2 cups of water to cook your minute rice
- 1 ½ cups spaghetti sauce
- 1/3 cup of onion diced
- 1 cup of mozzarella cheese shredded
- ½ teaspoon of garlic salt

Cooking Instructions

1. Add a bit of olive oil and select the Sauté function on your Instant Pot. Add the ground beef and onions. Make your minute rice on the stove.

2. Cook until meat is cooked and onions soften. Pour in your spaghetti sauce and rice, give everything a good stir. Turn off your Instant Pot and remove pot.

3. Transfer contents into a separate bowl and wash your pot. Return the pot into your Instant Pot and pour in 1 ½ cups of water.

4. Open your kitchen deluxe vegetable steamer basket and lower it into the Instant Pot. Cut off the tops of the bell peppers and remove seeds inside.

5. Place 4 bell peppers into your steamer basket so they fit snuggly. Add a bit of mozzarella cheese into the inside, bottom, of each bell pepper.

6. Spoon rice and ground beef mixture into peppers until each one is almost filled up. Add another bit of mozzarella cheese on the top of each pepper on top of the rice mixture.

7. Secure the Lid, ensure that the valve is on sealing position. Select the Manual function, cook on High Pressure for about 10 minutes.

8. When the time is up, do a quick pressure release. Use central ring hook to lift vegetable steamer out of the Instant Pot. Serve and enjoy.

Potato Corn Chowder

Preparation time: 10 minutes

Cooking time: 10 minutes

Total time: 20 minutes

Serves: 5 to 6

Ingredients

- 6 red potatoes diced
- 4 ears corn (kernels removed from cob, about 2 cups, can use frozen or canned)
- ¼ onion diced
- 3 cups of vegetable broth can use water but this is better
- ¾ cup of cheddar cheese
- 3 cups half and half
- 2 tablespoons of corn starch a bit more depending on how thick you want it
- 3 tablespoons of butter
- Pinch of salt

Cooking Instructions

1. Dice all the veggies, select the Sauté function on your Instant Pot. Add in butter until melted, add diced onions and cook until soft.

2. Add vegetable broth, diced potatoes, and corn removed from the cob. Then add pinch of salt.

3. Secure the Lid, ensure that the valve is on sealing position. Select the Manual function, cook on High Pressure for about 10 minutes.

4. When the time is up, do a quick pressure release and open the Lid carefully. Add a bit of water to your cornstarch in a cup to use as a thickener.

5. Add to the pot and stir. Select the Sauté function on your Instant Pot to allow mixture to boil.

6. Add half and half and cheese slowly, stir and serve when it has thickened a bit.

7. Serve and enjoy.

Apple Pie Steel Cut Oats

Preparation time: 5 minutes

Cooking time: 20 minutes

Total time: 25 minutes

Serves: 5 to 6

Ingredients

- 1 cup of steel cut oats
- 1-2 apples diced
- 1 ½ teaspoons of cinnamon
- ½ teaspoon of salt
- ¼ teaspoon of nutmeg fresh grated
- 3 cups of water

Cooking Instructions

1. Add in all the ingredients in your Instant Pot. Secure the Lid, ensure that the valve is on sealing position.

2. Select the Manual function, cook for about 5 minutes. When the time is up, allow it to release pressure naturally for about 10 minutes.

3. Then do a quick pressure release to get rid of the remaining pressure. Stir and remove pot from Instant Pot housing.

4. Serve with your favorite toppings and enjoy.

Creamy Macaroni and Cheese

Preparation time: 6 minutes

Cooking time: 4 minutes

Total time: 10 minutes

Serves: 7 to 8

Ingredients

- 1 pound of Pasta - (we use large elbow macaroni noodles)
- 4 cups of water
- 4 tablespoons of butter
- 2 teaspoons of kosher or sea salt
- ½ teaspoon of black pepper
- 1 cup of heavy cream
- 8 ounces of sharp cheddar cheese, shredded
- 8 ounces of Mexican or Colby jack blend cheese, shredded

Cooking Instructions

1. Pour pasta, water, salt, pepper and butter into your Instant Pot and give everything a good stir.

2. Secure the Lid, ensure that the valve is on sealing position. Select the Manual function, cook on High Pressure for about 4 minutes.

3. When the time is up, do a quick pressure release. Pour in both cheeses and cream and give everything a good stir.

4. Serve and enjoy.

CHAPTER 9: SOUPS & STEWS

Minestrone Soup

Preparation time: 12 minutes

Cooking time: 6 minutes

Total time: 18 minutes

Serves: 5 to 6

Ingredients

- 2 tablespoons of olive oil
- 2 stalks celery diced
- 1 large onion diced
- 1 large carrot diced
- 3 cloves of garlic minced
- 1 teaspoon of dried oregano
- 1 teaspoon of dried basil
- pepper to taste
- 28 ounces of san Marzano tomatoes
- 15 ounces can or about 2 cups freshly cooked, drained white or cannellini beans
- 4 cups of bone broth or vegetable broth
- 1 bay leaf
- ½ cup of fresh spinach or kale without the rib torn into shreds
- 1 cup of gluten-free elbow pasta
- 1/3 cup of finely grated parmesan cheese omit for vegan option
- 1-2 tablespoons of fresh pesto optional

Cooking Instructions

1. Select the Sauté function on your Instant Pot, add in olive oil, onion, carrot, celery and garlic. Mix until softened.

2. Add in basil, oregano, salt and pepper. If canned tomatoes are still whole, pulse tomatoes and liquid in can in a blender or food processor for a few seconds to dice tomatoes.

3. Add tomatoes, bone broth, spinach or kale, bay leaf, and pasta. Secure the Lid, select the Manual function, cook on High Pressure for about 6 minutes.

4. When the time is up, allow it to release pressure naturally for about 1 to 2 minutes. Then, do a quick pressure release.

5. Remove Lid carefully and add white kidney beans. Serve in bowls and garnish with parmesan cheese and a dollop of pesto.

6. Serve and enjoy.

Pot Borscht (Beet Soup)

Preparation time: 15 minutes

Cooking time: 15 minutes

Total time: 30 minutes

Serves: 3 to 4

Ingredients

- 1 medium white onion, chopped
- 1 tsp. of salt
- 2 tbsp. of olive oil
- 2 large white potatoes, peeled and diced into small cubes (about 1lb / 450 g)
- 1 large carrot, grated (about 4.5 oz/ 125 g)
- 2 medium beets or 3 small ones, grated (7-8 oz / 200-250 g)
- ¼ medium white cabbage, thinly sliced (12 oz / 350 g)
- 4 medium cloves of garlic, diced
- 10-12 g dried porcini mushrooms
- 3 tbsp. of apple cider vinegar
- 1.5 tbsp. of tomato paste
- 1 cube beef stock
- 1 cube vegetable stock
- ½ tsp. of pepper
- 1.25 litres filtered water (5 cups)
- Fresh parsley and sour cream/yoghurt to serve

Cooking Instructions

1. Select the Sauté function on your Instant Pot. Add the olive oil and onions and Sauté for about 2 minutes, until softened.

2. Add potatoes, carrots and beets, and give everything a good stir. Add the cabbage, garlic and the rest of the ingredients.

3. Stir through and Select the Keep Warm/Cancel button. Secure the Lid, ensure that the valve is on the sealing position.

4. Select the Manual function, cook on High Pressure for about 10 minutes. When the time is up, allow it to release pressure naturally for about 5 minutes.

5. Then, use the quick release to get rid of the remaining pressure. Serve the soup with chopped fresh parsley and a dollop of sour cream. Enjoy.

Chicken Noodle Soup

Preparation time: 20 minutes

Cooking time: 20 minutes

Total time 40 minutes

Serves: 5 to 6

Ingredients

- 4 whole chicken legs including thighs
- olive oil
- 4 carrots peeled and sliced
- 4 stalks celery sliced, including leaves
- 1 onion diced
- 3 cloves garlic minced
- 6 to 8 cups chicken stock
- 1 tsp. of ground turmeric
- 1 tbsp. of soy sauce
- 1 tbsp. of ginger grated
- 8 ounces of dried rice noodles
- 4 tbsp. of minced fresh parsley

Cooking Instructions

1. Take the chicken out of the fridge and Allow it sit on room temperature for about 20 minutes, salt and pepper the chicken, prepare the veggies.

2. Select the Sauté function on your Instant Pot and add a few swirls of olive oil. Add the chicken skin side down to the pan.

3. Allow the chicken to rest undisturbed for about 5 minutes to brown, turn and brown the other side.

4. Remove the chicken. If needed, add a bit more oil to the pot. Then add in the carrots, celery, onions and garlic to the pot and sauté until slightly softened.

5. Add the turmeric, soy sauce and grated ginger and about a cup of the stock. Stir and scrap up any brown bits on the bottom.

6. Top with the chicken and pour over the remaining stock. Secure the Lid, ensure that the valve is on sealing position.

7. Select the Manual function, cook for about 12 minutes. When the time is up, do a quick pressure release.

8. Remove the chicken and set aside to cool. Turn off your Instant Pot and select the sauté function on your Instant Pot.

9. When the soup comes up to a boil, add the noodles and cook for about 5 minutes. While the noodles are cooking, separate the chicken meat from the bones.

10. When the noodles are done, turn off the Instant Pot, and stir back in the chicken. Serve topped with the fresh parsley.

11. Serve and enjoy.

Chicken Meatball and Kale Soup

Preparation time: 10 minutes

Cooking time: 20 minutes

Total time: 30 minutes

Serves: 5 to 6

Ingredients

For the meatballs:

- 1 ½ pounds of ground chicken breast
- 2 tablespoons of arrowroot powder or ¼ cup panko breadcrumbs
- 1 teaspoon of salt
- 1 teaspoon of pepper
- ½ teaspoon of crushed red pepper (optional)
- 1 teaspoon of garlic powder
- 1 teaspoon of onion powder
- ½ tablespoon of dried oregano
- ½ tablespoon of basil
- 2 tablespoons of nutritional yeast or grated Parmesan cheese

For soup:

- 6 cups of low sodium vegetable stock
- 4 celery stalks, diced
- 2 medium onions, diced
- 3 medium carrots, peeled and diced
- 1 bunch kale, coarsely chopped
- 2 teaspoons of thyme
- 2 garlic cloves, minced
- 2 teaspoons of salt (or to taste)
- ½ teaspoon of crushed red pepper (or to taste)
- 2 tablespoons of olive oil
- 2 eggs, beaten (opt)

Cooking Instructions

1. (Make the soup base) select the High Sauté function on your Instant Pot and add olive oil and heat for about 1 minute.

2. Add celery, onions, and carrots. Sauté for about 3 minutes, until vegetables start to become soft.

3. Add in garlic, salt, thyme, and red pepper. Add in kale and give everything a good stir to combine. Add the vegetable stock and continue to cook.

4. (Make the meatballs) In a large bowl, combine all the ingredients for the meatballs and mix well.

5. Use a tbsp. to measure out meatballs. Wet hands to help create smooth balls and roll chicken mixture into meatballs.

6. Wet your hands, if you feel the chicken sticking to your hands. Add chicken to the soup by gently dropping into the cooking soup. (Do not stir) or the meatballs will break apart.

7. Cancel the sauté function using the cancel/keep warm button. Secure the Lid, select the Manual function, cook on High Pressure for about 15 minutes.

8. When the time is up, do a quick pressure release and return the soup to the sauté setting.

9. Slowly drizzle in beaten eggs in a circular motion throughout the pot and cook for about 2 minutes or until egg are set.

10. Turn off your Instant Pot. Serve with grated parmesan if desired.

11. Serve and enjoy.

Paleo Hamburger Soup

Preparation time: 10 minutes

Cooking time: 30 minutes

Total time: 40 minutes

Serves: 3 to 4

Ingredients

- 2 tbsp. of avocado oil
- 1 onion, diced
- 1 lb. of grass-fed ground beef
- 2 cups of chopped carrots
- 2 tbsp. of primal palate meat + potatoes seasoning
- 1 tsp. of sea salt
- 1 tbsp. of garlic powder
- 4 cups of beef broth (organic store bought or homemade)
- 5 medium Yukon gold potatoes (whole)

Cooking Instructions

1. Select the Sauté function on your Instant Pot drizzle in the avocado oil and onion. Allow the onions to cook for about 5 to 8 minutes, stirring them around so that they do not burn.

2. Add the ground beef and break it up a bit with a spatula, pour in the broth, add the seasonings and carrots and whole potatoes.

3. Close and lock the Lid in place, select the Keep Warm/Cancel button. Now select the Soup button and close the pressure valve.

4. Once it's done cooking, do a quick pressure release. Open the lid carefully and use a potato masher to break up the potatoes until they are made into small chunks

5. Serve and enjoy.

Egg Roll Soup

Preparation time: 10 minutes

Cooking time: 30 minutes

Total time: 40 minutes

Ingredients

- 1 tbsp. of (15ml) lard or extra virgin olive oil
- 1 lb. of (450g) ground pastured pork
- 1 large onion, diced
- 4 cups of (946ml) chicken or beef broth (Instant Pot tutorial here; I like this brand too)
- ½ head cabbage, chopped
- 2 cups of (680g) shredded carrots
- 1 tsp. of garlic powder
- 1 tsp. of onion powder
- 1 tsp. of unrefined finely ground salt
- 1 tsp. of ground ginger
- 2/3 cup of coconut aminos
- (Option) 2 to 3 tbsp. of tapioca starch

Cooking Instructions

1. In your Instant Pot, brown the ground pork in the tablespoon of cooking fat with the diced onion. Sauté until no longer pink.

2. Add the rest of the ingredients (except for the tapioca starch). Close and lock the lid in place. Select the Keep Warm/Cancel button.

3. Press the Soup button (high pressure for 30 minutes) and allow to cook. When the timer beeps, do a quick pressure release.

4. Carefully open the lid. If you want a thicker soup, remove 1/4 cup of broth from the soup and stir in 2-3 tablespoons of tapioca starch.

5. Add the slurry and give everything a good stir well to thicken. Serve and enjoy.

Thai Peanut Chicken Soup

Preparation Time: 10 minutes

Cook Time: 10 minutes

Total Time: 20 minutes

Yield: Serves 6

Ingredients

- 2 strips bacon, diced
- 1/2 cup onion, diced
- 1.5 cups sweet potato, diced
- 1 cup red pepper, diced
- 1 cup zucchini, diced
- 1 cup summer squash, diced
- 1 cup frozen corn kernals
- 1-2 tablespoon of fresh ginger
- 3 tablespoons of soy sauce
- 1.5 cups of chicken broth
- 1.5 lb. chicken breast, diced
- 1 teaspoon of paprika
- 1 can coconut milk (we used full fat)
- 1/4 cup of peanut butter
- Optional garnishes: green onions, chopped peanuts, sriracha

Cooking Instructions

1. Turn the Instant Pot to Sauté. Add bacon and onion and cook for about 3 minutes. Turn Instant Pot off.

2. Add the rest of the ingredients except coconut milk and peanut butter. Give everything a good stir to combine.

3. Close and lock the lid in place. Select Manual, High Pressure for 10 minutes. When the timer beeps, do a quick pressure release.

4. Carefully open the lid and add coconut milk and peanut butter. Stir to combine.

5. Serve warm with optional garnishes if desired.

Beef Stew with Potatoes

Preparation Time: 20 minutes

Cook Time: 1 hour

Servings: 5

Ingredients

- 1 1/2 lb. chuck roast or beef stew meat cut into 1-2 inch chunks
- 16 oz. bag frozen pearl onions
- 8 oz. carrots about 3, peeled and chopped into 1 inch chunks
- 1 lb. Russet potato about 1 large, peeled and chopped into 1 inch chunks
- 10 oz. mushrooms, quartered
- 2 cups of beef stock
- 3 tbsp. of tomato paste
- 3 tbsp. of all-purpose flour
- 1 tbsp. of butter
- 1 tsp. of salt

Cooking Instructions

1. In a medium bowl, toss beef chunks with flour until coated. Select the sauté function on your Instant Pot and add the butter to melt.

2. Add beef chunks. Sauté until browned on all sides, about 5 minutes, stirring frequently. Add beef broth to the pot, stirring well.

3. Add salt and tomato paste, stirring until dissolved. Add the rest of the ingredients (frozen pearl onions, carrots, potatoes, mushrooms) to the pot. Stir.

4. Close and lock the lid in place. Press the Meat/Stew function and set the cooking time to 35 minutes.

5. When the timer beeps, do a natural pressure release for about 10 minutes. Carefully open the lid and stir.

6. Taste and add additional salt if needed. Serve hot and optionally garnish with chopped parsley.